THE DIVINE LAW

RELIGION AND CHRISTIANITY

From Religion than came Judaism;
From Judaism than cam Christianity.
"If you want a good understanding
from a historical perspective,
this is the book for you".

Reverend Lawrence L. Blankenship

iUniverse, Inc.
New York   Bloomington

The Divine Law
Religion and Christianity

For information or to order additional books, please write:
The Divine Law
P.O. Box 2971
Pensacola, Florida 32513-2971
U.S.A.

Or visit our website at thedivinelaw.com/rblankenship80@yahoo.com

iUniverse books may be ordered through booksellers or by contacting:

iUniverse
1663 Liberty Drive
Bloomington, IN 47403
www.iuniverse.com
1-800-Authors (1-800-288-4677)

ISBN: 978-1-4502-6179-1 (sc)
ISBN: 978-1-4502-6180-7 (ebk)

Printed in the United States of America

iUniverse rev. date: 10/18/2010

Contents

Acknowledgments

At this very moment, wave of people believe in Christianity fervor is sweeping the world. And, the United States, our preachers, members, and community are increasing likely to be devout followers of Christians, tradition are familiar to us.

At no other time in history has it seemed more people understand Christianity. What, specifically, do the followers believe? How do they view those who not share their understanding God and Jesus Christ?

The fourth edition of The Divine Law: Religion and Christianity is a major revision that strives to achieve the shared goal of the previous editions to present a clear, relevant, and balanced history of the United States, and the world; an unfolding story of national development, from the days of the earliest inhabitants to the present. In each Chapter, we sought to blend the excitement and drama of the American experience with in sights about the social, economic, and cultural history that underlie it.

The author is deeply indebted and sincerely grateful to many individuals for their suggestions and criticisms in the preparation of the manuscript, namely, late Rev. E. D. Blankenship Sr.,[his Father]; Dr. Herbert J. Vandort; Rev. Johnnie J. Blocker; Mrs. Willie L. Blankenship[his Mother]; Sis. Zennie M. Blocker; Ms. Katie M. Reese; Ms. La'Rhonda B. Smith[his daughter]; Ms. Lucille French [his daughter]; and Ms. Helen Nixon, who gave him the benefit of their comments and criticisms after either reading the manuscript or using the preliminary edition as a text in their lives; and certain unknown reviewers for their evaluation and criticism. Finally, the author owes no greater debt of appreciation and gratitude than due [his Mother], and [his Wife] Zelmer J. Blankenship, and his wife encouraged through the months of writing and rewriting necessary to get it in its final form.

Reverend Lawrence L. Blankenship

Introduction

All social movements involve conflicts which are reflected intellectually in controversies. It would not be a sign of health if such an important social interest as religion not an arena of struggles, practical and theoretical. But for theory, at least for the theory that forms a philosophy of Christianity, the practical conflicts and the controversies that are conducted upon the level of these conflicts, only set a problem. It is the business of an intelligent theory of Christianity to ascertain the cause for the conflicts that exist and then, instead of taking one side or the other, to indicate a plan of operations proceeding from a level deeper and more inclusive than is represented by the practices and ideas of the contending parties.

This formulation of the business of the philosophy of Christianity does not mean that the mentioned, should attempt to bring about a compromise between opposed churches of thought, to find a via media, nor yet make an eclectic combination of points picked out hither and you from all churches. It means the necessity of a new order of conceptions leading to new modes of practice. It is for this reason that it is so difficult to develop a philosophy of Christianity, the moment tradition and custom are departed from. It is for this reason that the conduct of church, based upon a new order of conceptions, is so much more difficult than is the management of church which walk in beaten path. Hence, every movement in the direction of a new order of ideas and of activities directed by them calls out, sooner or later, a return to what appear to be simpler and more fundamental ideas and practices of the past, as is exemplified at present in education in the attempt to revive the principles of ancient Greece and of the middle ages.

It is in this context that I have suggested at the close of this little volume that those who are looking ahead to a new movement in Christianity, adapted to the existing need for a new social order, should think in terms of Christianity itself rather than in terms of some 'ism about Christianity' , even such an 'ism as progressivism'. For in spite of itself any movement that thinks and acts in terms of an 'ism becomes so involved in reaction against' other 'isms that it is unwittingly controlled by them'. For it then forms its principles by reaction against them instead of by a comprehensive constructive survey of actual needs, problems, and possibilities. Whatever value is possessed by the essay presented in this little volume resides in its attempt to call attention to the larger and deeper issues of Christian so as to suggest their proper frame of reference.

Reverend Lawrence L. Blankenship

CHAPTER 1

Religion and Christianity

Mankind likes to think in terms of extreme opposites. It is formulating its beliefs in terms of Religion or Christianity, which it recognizes no intermediate possibilities. When forced to recognize that the extremes cannot be acted upon, it is still inclined to held that they are all right in theory but that when it comes to practical matters circumstances compel us to compromise. Christianity philosophy is no exception. The history of Christianity theory is marked by opposition between the idea that Christian is development from within and that it is formation from without; that it is based upon natural endowments and that Christian is a process of overcoming natural inclination and substituting in its place habits acquired under external pressure. At present, the opposition, so far as practical affairs of the church are concerned, tends to take the form of contrast between Religion and Christianity. If the underlying ideas of the former are formulated broadly, without the qualifications required for accurate statement, they are found to be about as follows: (1) the subject matter of Christian is a person related is some way to Jesus Christ. The word is often used of members of the Church; this would lead to debate about what bodies should be included in the concept of the Church. (2) the subject of Religious is the study may best be thought of as a system embodying the means of attaining and expressing in conduct the values deemed characteristic of the ideal life including concepts of belief in sacred rites, sacrifices, offerings, duly,

1

and worship. Remember, the subject matter of Christian consists of bodies of believer and of skills that have been worked out in the past; therefore, the chief business of the church is to transmit them to the New Generation. In the past, there have also been developed standards and rules of conduct; moral training consists in forming habits of action in conformity with these rules and standards. Finally, the general pattern of church organization, by which I mean the relations of pupils to one another and to the teachers, constitutes the church a kind of institution sharply marked off from other social institutions. Call up in imagination the ordinary church, its time schedules, schemes of classification, of examination and promotion, of rules of order, and I think you will grasp what is meant by pattern of beliefs organization. If then you contrast this scene with what goes on in the family, for example, you will appreciate what is meant by the church being a kind of institution sharply marked off from any other form of social organization. The three characteristics just mentioned fix the aims and methods of instruction and discipline. The main purpose or objective is to prepare the young for future responsibilities and for success in life, by means of acquisition of the organized bodies of information and prepared forms of skill which comprehend the material of instruction. Since the subject matter as well as standards of proper conduct are handed down from the past, the attitude of pupils must, upon the whole, be one of docility, receptivity, and obedience. Books, especially textbooks, are the chief representatives of the lore and wisdom of the past, while teachers are the organs through which pupils are brought into effective connection with the material. Teachers are the agents through which knowledge and skills are communicated and rules of conduct enforced. I have not made this brief summary for the purpose of criticizing the underlying philosophy. The rise of what is called New Religious and Christian church is of itself a product of discontent with traditional education. I effect it is a criticism of the latter. When the implied criticism is made explicit it reads somewhat as follows: the traditional scheme is, in essence, one of imposition from above and from outside. It imposes adult standards subject matter, and methods upon those who are only growing slowly toward maturity. The gap is so great that the required subject matter, the methods of leaning and of having are foreign to the existing capacities of the young. They are beyond the reach of the experience the young learners already possess. Consequently, they must be imposed; even though good teachers will use devices of art to cover up the imposition so as to relieve it of obviously brutal features. But the gulf between the mature or adult products and the experience and abilities of the people is so wide that the very situation forbids much active participation by pupils. There is to do and learn, as it was the part of the six hundred to do and die. Learning here means acquisition of what already is incorporated in books and in the heads of the elders. Moreover, that which is taught is thought of as essentially static. It is taught as a finished product, with little regard either to ways in which it was originally built up to changes that will surely occur in the future would be much like the past, and yet it is used as educational food in a society where change is the rule, not the exception. If one attempts to formulate the philosophy of Christian implicit in the practices of the newer Christianity, we may, I think, discover certain common principles amid the variety of religion Church now existing. To imposition from above is opposed expression and cultivation of individuality; to external discipline is opposed free activity; to learning from texts and teachers, learning through experience; to acquisition of isolated skills and techniques by drill, is opposed acquisition of them as means of attaining ends which make direct vital appeal; to preparation for a more or less remote future is opposed making the most of the opportunities of present life; to static aims and materials is opposed acquaintance with a changing world. Now, all by themselves are abstract. They become concrete only in the consequences which result from their application. Just because the principles set forth are so fundamental and far-reaching, everything depends upon the interpretation given them as they are put into practice in the church and the home. It is at this point that the reference made earlier to Christian philosophies becomes peculiarly pertinent. The general philosophy of the New Christianity may be sound, and yet the difference in abstract principles will not decide the way in which the moral and intellectual preference involved shall be worked out in practice. There is always the danger in a new movement that in rejecting aims and methods of that which it would supplant, it may develop its principles negative rather than positively and constructively. Then it takes its clew in practice from that which is rejected instead of from the constructive development of its own philosophy. I take it that the fundamental unity of the newer philosophy is found in the idea that there is an intimate and necessary relation between the processes of actual experience and education. If this be true, then a positive and constructive development of its own basic idea depends upon having a correct idea of experience.

Take, the question of organized Christianity matter, which will be discussed in some detail later. The problem for Religion education is; the characteristic of the various religions differ so widely that it may be impossible, by this method, to find any common features, or, if any are found, they must be so vague as to be of doubtful value. Such a method would yield, as definitive characteristic of religion, the acknowledgment of a higher, unseen power; and attitude of reverent dependence on that power in the conduct of life; and special actions, rites, prayers, acts mercy etc., as peculiar expressions, and means of cultivation of the religious attitude. How does religion matter function? Is there anything inherent in experience which tends towards religious organization of its contents? What results follow when the materials of experience are not religious organized? A philosophy which proceeds on the basis of rejection, of sheer opposition, will neglect these questions. It will tend to suppose that because the Old Religion was based on ready made organization, therefore it suffices to reject the principle of organization in too, instead of striving to discover what it means and how it is to be attained on the basis of experience. We might go through all the points of difference between the Religious and Christian education, and reach similar conclusions. When external control is rejected, the problem becomes that of finding the factors of control that are inherent within experience. When external authority is rejected, it does not follow that all authority should be rejected but rather that there is need to search for a more effective source of authority. Because the religious education imposed the knowledge, methods, and the rules of conduct of the mature person upon the young, it does not follow, except upon the basis of the extreme Christian philosophy, that the knowledge and skill of the mature person has no directive value for the experience of the immature. On the contrary, Christian education upon personal experience may mean more multiplied and more intimate contacts between the mature and the immature than ever existed in the traditional church, and consequently more, rather than less, guidance by others. The problem then, is, how these contacts can be established without violating the principle of learning through personal experience. The solution of the problem requires a well thought out philosophy of the social factors that operate in the constitution of individual experience. What is indicated in the foregoing remarks is that the general principles of the New Christian do not of themselves solve any of the problems of the actual or practical conduct and management of schools. Rather, they set new problems which have to be worked out on the basis of a Christian experience. The problems are not even recognized to say nothing of being solved, when it is assumed that it suffices to reject the ideas and practices of the Old Religion and then go to the opposite extreme. Yet, I am sure that you will appreciate what is meant when I say that many of the newer church tend to make little or nothing of organized subject matter of Christian; to proceed as if any form of direction and guidance by adults were an invasion of individual freedom, and as if the idea that Christianity should be concerned with the present and future meant that acquaintance with the past has little or not role to play in Christianity. Without pressing these defects to the point of exaggeration, they at least illustrate what is meant by a theory and practice of Christian which proceeds negatively or by reaction against which proceeds negatively or by reaction against what has been current in Christian rather than by a positive and constructive development of purposes, methods, and subject matter on the foundation of a theory of experience and its Christianity potentialities.

It is not too much to say that an Christian philosophy which professes to be based on the idea of Christianity may become as dogmatic as ever was the religious theory which is reacted against. For any theory and set of practices is dogmatic which is not based upon critical examination of its own underlying principles. Let us say that the New Christian emphasizes the Christian of the learner. A problem is now set. What does Christian mean, "a person related in some way to the Lord Jesus Christ". If you are a Christian you have freedom mean and what are the conditions under imposition which was so common in the traditional church limited rather than promoted the intellectual and moral development of the young and old recognition of this serious defect sets a problem. Just what is the role of the religion teacher and of books in promoting the educational development of the immature? Admit, that religion teacher as the subject matter for study facts and ideas so bound up with the past as to give little help in dealing with the issues of the present, and future. Very well, now we have the two of discovering the connection exists within experience between the religion and Christianity of the past and the issues of the present. We have the problem of ascertaining how acquaintance with the past may be translated into a potent instrumentality for dealing effectively with the future. We may reject knowledge of the past as the end of religious and thereby only emphasize its importance as a means. When shall the young become acquainted with the past in such a way that the acquaintance is a potent minister in appreciation of the living present? As I wrote on page three(3)paragraph two (2) "Christianity" matter which will be discussed in some detail. The necessity of starting from the thought of the Christian faith and life within the church as an organic whole might suggest that nothing less than an exposition of the whole content of the faith is required if we are to understand the significance and authority of the Bible within it. Fortunately that is not so. Just because we are dealing with an organic whole, and are particularly interested in the normative factors within it, all that is required is a grasp of that central and controlling truth which imparts and preserves to the whole its specifically Christian character, distinguishing it once and for all from other religious matter, no matter what partial identities or similarities there may otherwise be.

There can hardly be division of opinion as to what this central and controlling, essence of Christian faith and life is. It is belief in the Incarnation, the conviction that God himself came, and comes, into human history in the person of Jesus Christ. Jesus Christ is God himself in action within history "for us men, women, children, and for our salvation", in a way that is unique, final, adequate, and indispensable. There is none other name under heaven given among men, women, and children, whereby we must be saved". Act. 4:12 reads, "Neither is there salvation in any other: for there is none other name under heaven given among men, whereby we must be saved". Remember, God so loved the world, that he gave his only begotten Son". God was in Christ, reconciling the world unto himself. II Cor. 5:19. There have, of course, been great differences among Christians as to the precise significance

6

and implications of this central affirmation of the Incarnation, the grounds for making it, the way in which the divine action it describes is wrong out in men, women, and children live; and some have interpreted it in ways that have seemed to others destructive of its distinctively Christian meaning. But it hardly can be questioned that unless a man is prepared to make the affirmation in some sense or other, then, no matter how much he may in fact owe to Christian teaching, or may accept and exemplify Christian moral values, any claim he may make to be a specifically Christian believer, with a specifically Christian gospel to preach, is to say the least, extremely dubious. This is not a merely personal view; on the contrary, it is hardly more that a report of evident historical truth. However much and rightly we may dislike heresy hunting, and whatever difficult may arise in border line cases, the fact remains that the belief in the Incarnation has been the central, distinctive, all controlling belief of the Christian movement the ages; it is the heart and soul of what may be called New Christian, meaning by that simply Christian as a movement having a distinctive character and being identifiable as such, in spite of all its variant and even conflicting forms, throughout the centuries.

The statement of the dogma of the Incarnation just made, that God, himself came, and comes, into human history in the person of Jesus Christ, does not, however, suffice without further explication to bring out the distinctive essence of the Christian faith as this is determinative of the significance and authority of the Bible within it. Remember page three (3) church has regarded the Scriptures as being in some sense the special revelation of God, and therefore as being in some sense the final standard or norm of Christian truth. The Old Testament seems to have been accepted from the beginning as an authoritative revelation of God, and it was not very long before the writings which came ultimately to form the New Testament were also in circulation, carrying a similar, though not precisely assessed authority. No consistent or unanimous answer has, however, been given by the church to the question in what sense exactly the Scriptures are the revelation of God and the standard of truth. This article is intended to be a contribution to the answering of this question as it confront the Christian believer today. It is written from the Holy Bible of Christian faith and experience as these are shared and known within the fellowship of the Christian church; that is to say, it accepts as a datum the uniquely normative status which the church has always assigned to the Holy Bible, and it endeavors to explore its meaning and bearings in relation to the Christian faith taken as whole. In other words, the question of the Bible is here considered as a theological question; the answering of it involves raising the question as to what the Christian faith essentially is, for only on that basis can we determine the essential significance and authority of the Bible. It is, of course, possible to approach the Bible from other angles in relation to other interests and beliefs. The books of the Bible are so various, and cover alike in their origin and content so vest a period of time, that they provide invaluable material for the historian, the archaeologist, the anthropologist, and many others. Each of these, in using the biblical material, asks and answers the question of the significance and authority of the Bible for his particular study. Such different approaches may provide important material for the Christian theologian inquiring into the significance and authority of the Bible for the Christian faith; indeed, there is no reason why the Christian theologian himself should not no occasion study the Bible, not as a theologian, but as a historian, an archaeologist, or an anthropologist. The question whether in pursuing such studies he should seek to de-vest himself of his Christian conviction and presuppositions we need not explore. The point is that however, much the various ways of studying the Bible may interact, the special interest of the Christian theologian as such, and the one which governs this article, remains quite distinct. We raise the question of the significance and authority of the Bible as part of the wider theological question of the essence of the Christian faith which the church is commissioned to proclaim to the world.

The purpose of this book review of the central content of the Bible as seen through Christianity of the New Testament is to make clear at the outset what the chief task of biblical theology must be. That task is simply to expound the meaning and implications of the biblical creed in its various forms. This must be done in as coherent, reflective, and relevant a manner as possible, to the end that the Gospel may be preach in and by the church with clarity and power. It must further be stated that the Christian in approaching the Old Testament inevitably does so with certain presuppositions which he must confess. These involve the conviction that Jesus Christ is both the destination of and the guide to the Old Testament's basic content. This does not mean that the Christian is entitled to betray the Old Testament by reading into it meanings which are not there, nor that he can neglect the most rigid use of the tools of scholarship, learning shown by a minister or student standard of academic work. Yet it does mean that he or she performs his or her scholarly and exegetical work in the knowledge of God's fulfilled time, and with the conviction that Christian faith in its deeper dimensions is an integral part of her or her own faith through the New Christianity of which he or she is a member by faith in Jesus Christ. Such a definition of our task and of its presuppositions is, however, far too simple unless it recognizes the many difficulties which lie in the way of a biblical theology or of a theology of either both Testaments. By its very nature theology involves an attempt to systematize and generalize by means of abstract language.

Yet biblical religion is a living faith which can never be confined in generalizations nor in an abstract system. It is based upon an anthropomorphic vocabulary which, when translated into abstractions, loss its creative power. Its central content is a historical creed, the ramifications of which are many and various in the complexities of a long history and of various schools, and university of thought within that history. Yet the task of the church demands that we must make the attempt to organize the central articles of the faith, to penetrate behind them in order to discover their foundations, and to portray as well as we can their historical developments and ramifications. This the church has done repeatedly, as it was done in each generation of biblical history itself. Thus while at times our gait may be a bit unsteady, we must proceed in the faith that God himself will verify and validate His truth, even though our own attempts to express and expound it are incomplete and historically conditioned. Remember, we are Christian. It is impossible to give an exact definition of the word. In the strictest sense it would be applied to one who has a true, saving faith in Jesus Christ, but only God Himself has a certain knowledge as to who the true believers are. The word is often used of members of the church; this would lead to debate about what bodies should be included in the concept of the church. It is often used laxly in the sense of "Christlike", applicable to persons who make no pretense of being believers in Jesus Christ in a religious sense but who admire and try to copy some features of his character. As I previous stated that, "We are Christian". The Christian movement began on Jewish land and made its first converts among the Sons of Israel, whose name was Jacob. Those who adhered to the new faith differed from their Jews in that they believe that Jesus of Nazareth was the Messiah and that God had vindicated his claim by raising him from the dead. The ties with Judaism were not completely cut, but persecution drove an ever deepening wedge between the two groups. Before Judaic Christian dwindled into comparative insignificance, it passed on its heritage to the Gentiles, who were reached through Greek speaking Jews such as Barnabas and Paul. The beginnings of Judaism was restriction of sacrifice to Jerusalem by Josiah, the destruction of the temple in 586 B. C., and the growing dispersion of Jewry both east and west meant a fundamental change in religious outlook. Though theoretically the cult in Jerusalem remained the center of Jewish religion, at least eight percent of the people were not able to make effective use of it. The only one of the many attempted answers to this problem that concerns us here was the making of a strict observance of the law the major concern of all Jews. We much understand Judaism Christian; the term is sometime used of every form of Christian belief after the destruction of Solomon's temple in 586 B. C. It seem better to confine it to the period beginning with the destruction of Herod's temple in A. D. 70, except where the phenomena under discussion can be clearly traced back to the interestsmental period. In this article, unless the context clearly demands otherwise it will be further restricted to that form of Judaism which from the beginning of the third century A.D., to the middle of the nineteenth held the loyalty of all but an insignificant fraction of the Jewish people. Where it is necessary to distinguish it from other forms of Judaism, it is generally called Rabbinic, Traditional and Orthodox. There is no evidence that the teaching of the Old Testament had not been understood, that they are not all Israel, which are of Israel. The five books of Moses, or Torah, to be rendered instruction rather than law, were regarded as the perfect and final revelation of God. The Prophets were only a commentary on them made necessary by man's sins. Though the whole of the Old Testament is of unquestioned authority, the inspiration of the Torah has always been placed higher than that of the Prophets or the Writings. Some scholar has regarded it as merely an earthly copy of a heavenly original, antedating creation and an agent in it, for whose sake man was created. These developments were deliberate efforts to make the Torah a counterweight to the person of Jesus Christ. The bulk of religious Jews have accommodated themselves to a greater or less extent to the world in which they live. The conservative Jew has trimmed away those commandments which seem to have lost their meaning. The Reform Jew like "Liberal" places the prophets before the Torah and retains only those customs of the past which he or she rationalize. It is probable that the majority of Jews are effectively atheist, whether they keep up a link with the synagogue or not. Among them nationalism "Zionism", has been the great substitute for religious, and it has influenced even many who think of themselves as religious. As I stated that Barnabas and Paul heritage to the Gentiles, who were reached through Greek speaking Jews. Christian is first mentioned in Acts. 11 :26 says: "And when he had found him, he brought him unto An' ti-och. And it came to pass, that a whole year they assembled themselves with the church, and taught much people. And the disciples were called "Christians first in Antioch". This is connection with the ministry of Barnabas and Paul at Antioch. Evidently the name soon spread beyond the Antioch of A. D., 40- 44, for it is used in the first General Epistle of Peter. 4:16 says: "Yet if a man suffer as a Christian, let him not be ashamed; but let him glorify God on this behalf". As though widely understood, its use by Agrippa to Paul in Acts. 26:1 says: "Then Agrippa, said unto Paul, thou art permitted to speak for thyself. Then Paul stretched forth the hand, and answered for himself". Paul defended himself of Christianity, may or may not have been in derision. Historically, Christian came to designate not a sect of Judaism, but a separate religion based on the person of Jesus Christ, rather than on a book of law, a dogma, or an institution. Remember, Christianity, though rooted in Judaism in Matthew. 5:17 says: "Think not that I am come to destroy the law, or the prophets: I am not come to destroy, but to fulfil". This is an entirely "New Christianity" and "New Song" , as David say in Psalms. 33:3-4 says: "Sing unto him a new song; play skifully with a loud noise. For the word of the Lord is right; and all his works are done in truth. Ezekiel. 36:26 says: "A new heart also will I give you, and a new spirit will I put within you: and I will take away the stony heart out of your flesh, and I will give you an heart of flesh". It is a revelation of God through His Son Jesus Christ, a way of life based on a personal experience of Jesus Christ. Obedience to his commandments, and a determination to increase your faith in Jesus Christ. John 15:10-11 says : "If ye keep my commandments, ye shall abide in my love; even as I have kept my Father's commandments, and abide in his love. These things have I spoken unto you, that my joy might remain in you, and that your joy might be full". As I stated that, we are Christian. For Old Testament teach may best be thought of as a system embodying the means of attaining and expressing in conduct the values deemed characteristic of the ideal life, including concepts of belief in sacred rites, sacrifices, and offerings. In Jewish and Christian thought religion is man's recognition of his relation to God and his expression of that relation in faith, worship, and conduct. Part of the inheritance of Christianity from Judaism was a Scripture. Jesus in his preaching constantly referred to this Scripture, and the disciples followed him in this practice. They accepted as religious fact which directly concerned them the existence among the Jews of a body of writings received as sacred and authoritative. This body of writings did not profess to include all the religious books that had appeared during the history of the Jewish people. It did not include all the religion documents which were in circulation among the Jews at that period. It was a body of writings which had been brought together by a process of selection, given an authority not possessed by their other religious literature, and invested with a sanctity which set it apart as in some particular way connected with the official religious life of the people. In this there was nothing unique. We find the same factors at work among other peoples producing the sacred books of other religions. As in the case as the "Menichaen" Scriptures, this religion philosophy taught from the 3rd century to the 7th century A.D., which were produced in conscious imitation of an earlier Canonical Scripture, we find that he Scripture of a religion consists of a body of writing of different age and authorship, formed by a gradual process of selection, and little by little acquiring sanctity and authority. The writings assembled in such sacred books are of various kinds, some historical, some didactic, some hortatory, some perhaps magical, but they gain their authority because the community feels that in them is enshrined something that is of vital significance for the practice of the religion whose sacred books they are. The Christians took over from the Jews this collection of sacred writings, and later formed an additional collection of their own, which in turn came to acquire sanctity and authority. With the development of the church, and the use of these documents as standards of doctrine and discipline, Christian writers began to make use of the Greek word "Kavwv" in a technical sense, and to speak of a canon of Scripture. Though the use of the word "Canon" in connection with an authoritative body of Scripture is a Christian origin, the conception which it crystallized in a convenient technical term was in operation long before any precise term was used. We have the conception wherever in a religious community there comes into existence a collection of writings marked off as especially sacred and authoritative, and so in modern books we speak of the Zoroastrian canon, or the Taoist canon, and distinguish in Buddhism between the Sanskrit, Pali, Tibetan, and Chinese canons. In none of these religions is the term used in the native sources, but the conception is there. When in any religion the stage is reached where the community is conscious that the authentic voice of religious authority is no longer heard, the writings which had been produced in that past in which such an authentic voice had been heard and recognized tend to be marked out by that fact and so to be set a side as the writings sacred to the community. This would not preclude the possibility of adding to them at some future time other peoples in which once again the sure voice religious authority was heard nor indeed of the adding to them of historical records, or memorials of past of the community, without which much of the meaning of the word of prophecy might be lost. Furthermore, the is not incompatible with some diversity of opinion as to the extent of such a corpus of sacred peoples, as to what should be included and what omitted.

What Christian theologians may recognize in the process of Scriptural canonization the official act of the church and the providential work of the Holy Spirit, and the Holy Bible. Its significance historians can merely state that a canon of Scripture is not something given, but something humanly devised. From the historical point of view the canon is the result of human decision as to which among the religious people existing in a community are those in which it recognizes the authentic voice of religious authority speaking to man. It is likewise clear that canonization is something entirely part from the process of collection, and that it is not necessarily connected with the public use of a body of writings. We have ample evidence of the collection and use in a community of religious people which have never become part of any canonical collection of Scripture. In general it is the effort to preserve the community from some threat to its religious life, whether from heresy or false teaching or some such calamity, that leads it to place the seal of its approval on certain people to the exclusion of others, already collected and in use, as being those alone in which it recognizes the authentic voice of authority. It is possible to think of a wider and a narrower sense of the word "canonization" which mean "Saint". It may be argued that a collection of people may come into use in a religious community and by custom and general recognition come to be regarded as of religious authority, without there ever having been any formal pronouncement as to its canonization. In this wider sense we could speak of a growing canon, as at different periods we find different groups of people attaining an authoritative position. In the stricter sense, however, canonization means a definite formulation whereby a body of people is set aside because those people are recognized as authoritative. In spite of these different of Religion and Christianity, we are versions are useful tools to the student of the Old Testament, providing us with valuable evidence on such important matters as text, exegesis, and canon. We are not "Religion", but we are "Christian".

CHAPTER 2

The Theory of Religious

In the beginning, the point we are making is the rejection of the philosophy and practice of traditional religious sets a new type of difficult belief problem for those who believe in the new type of Religion. We shall operate blindly and in confusion until we recognize this facts; until we thoroughly appreciate that departure from the old solves no problems what is said in the following pages is, accordingly, intended to indicate some of the main problems with which the newer Religious and to suggest the main lines along which their solution is to be sought.

We assume that amid all uncertainties there is one permanent frame of reference: namely, the organic connection between and Christianity; or that the philosophy of Religion is committed to some kind of empirical and experimental philosophy. But experience Religion and experiment are not self explanatory ideas. Rather, their meaning is part of the problem to be explored. To know the meaning of empiricism we need to understand what Christian experience are. The belief that all genuine religion comes about through experience does not mean that all experience genuinely or equally educative. Experience Christian and Religion cannot be directly equated to each other. For some regarding religion. Any experience is mis-belief regarding Religion or Christianity that has the effect of arresting or distorting the growth of further experience. An experience may be such as to engender callousness; it may produce lack of sensitivity and of responsiveness. Then the possibility of having experience Christian in the future are restricted. Again, a given experience Christian may increase a person's automatic skill in a particular direction and yet tend to land him or her in a groove or rut; the effect again is to narrow the field of further experience. An religion may be immediately enjoyable and yet promote the formation of a slack and careless attitude; this attitude then operates to modify the quality of subsequent experiences so as to prevent a person from getting out of them what they have to give. Remember, experiences may be so disconnected from one another that, while each is agreeable or even exciting in itself, they are not linked cumulatively to one another. Energy is then dissipated and a person becomes scatterbrained. Each experience may be lively, vivid, and "interesting", and yet their disconnectedness may artificially generate dispersive, disintegrated, centrifugal habits. The consequence of formation of such habits is inability to control future experiences. They are then taken, either by way of enjoyment or of discontent and revolt, just as they come. Under such circumstances, it is idle to talk of self control. Religion education offers a plethora of examples of experiences of the kinds just mentioned. It is a great mistake to suppose, even tacitly, that The religion teacher was not a place in which a adult or young person had experiences. Yet this is tacitly assumed when progressive education as a plan of learning by experience is placed in sharp opposition to the adult and young alike. The proper line of attack is that the experiences which were had, by young person and teachers alike, were largely of a wrong kind. How many young persons, for example, were rendered callous to ideas, and how many lost the impetus to learn because of the way in which learning was experienced by then? How many acquired special skills by means of automatic drill so that their power of judgment and capacity to act intelligently in new situation was limited? How many came to associate the learning process with a feeling of weariness and dissatisfaction and boredom? How many found what they did learn so foreign to the situations of life outside the church as to give them no power of control over the more recent situations? How many came to associate books or booklet with dull, drudgery, so that they were conditioned, to all but flashy reading matter? If I ask these questions, it is not for the sake of wholesale condemnation of the religion teacher. It is for quite another purpose. It is to emphasize the fact, first, that young people in religion institution do have experiences; and secondly, that the trouble is not the absence of experiences, but their defective and wrong character, wrong and defective from the standpoint of connection with further experience. The positive side of this point is even more important in connection with progressive education. It is not enough to insist upon the necessity of experience, nor even of activity in experience. Everything depends upon the quality of the experience has two aspects. There is an immediate aspect of agreeableness and there is its influence upon later Christians. The first is obvious and easy to judge. The Bible says, "we judge records to righteousness". The effect of an Christian is not borne on its face. It sets a problem to the preach or clergyman. It is his belief to arrange for the kind of Christianity which, while they do not repel the person, but rather engage his activities are, nevertheless, more than immediately enjoyable since they promote having desirable future Christians. Just as no man or woman lives or dies to themselves, so no Christians lives and dies to itself. Wholly independent of desire or intent, every experience lives on in further experiences. Hence the central problem of an religion based upon experience is to select the kind of present experiences that live fruitfully and creatively in subsequent experiences.

Later, I shall discuss in more detail the principle of the continuity of experience or what may be called the "Spirituality Continuum". Here I wish simply to emphasize the importance of this principle for the philosophy of spiritual experience. A philosophy of religious, like any theory, has to be stated in words, in belief. But so far as it is more than verbal it is a belief for conducting religious. Like any belief, it must be framed with reference to what is to be done and how it is to be done. The more definitely and sincerely it is held that religion is a development within, by, and for experience, the more important it is that there shall be clear conceptions of what experience is. Unless experience is so conceived that the result is a belief for deciding upon subject matter, upon methods of instruction, and discipline, and upon teacher, and social organization of the church or congregation, or temple, or synagogue, it is wholly in the air. It is reduced to a form of words which may be emotionally stirring but for which any other set of words might equally well be substituted unless they indicate operations to be initiated and executed. Just because traditional religion was a matter of routine in which the belief and programs were handed down from the past, present, and future, it does not follow that progressive religious is a matter of belief less improvisation. The traditional religion could get along without any consistently developed philosophy of religion. About all it required in that line was a set of abstract words like culture, discipline, or self-control, our great cultural heritage, etc, actual guidance being derived not from them but from custom and established routines. Just because progressive religious cannot rely upon established traditions and institutional habits, they must either proceed more or less chance or be directed by ideas which, when they are made articulate and coherent, from a philosophy of religion. Revolt against the kind of organization characteristic of the traditional religion constitutes a demand for a kind of organization based upon ideas. I think that only slight acquaintance with the history of religion is need to prove that religious reformers and innovators alone have felt the need for philosophy of religion.

Those who adhered to the established system needed merely a few fine sounding words to justify existing practices. The real work was done by habits which were so fixed as to be institutional. The lesson for progressive religious is that it requires in an urgent degree, a degree more pressing than was incumbent upon former innovators, a philosophy of religion based upon a philosophy of experience. I remarked incidentally that some philosophy in question is, to paraphrase the saying of some scholar about religion, one of religion, by, and for experience.

No one of these words, Belief, Faith, and Practices, names anything which is self-evident. Each of them is a challenge to discover and put into operation a principle of order and organization which follows from understanding what religion experience signifies. It is accordingly, a much more difficult task to work out the kinds of materials, of methods, and of social relationships that are appropriate to the new ideas than is the case with traditional religion. I think many of the difficulties experienced in the conduct of progressive religious and many of the criticisms leveled against them arise from this source. The difficulties are aggravated and the criticisms are increased when it is supposed that the new idea is somehow easier than the old. This belief is, I imagine, more or less current. Perhaps it illustrates again the either or philosophy, springing from the idea that about all which is required is not to do what is done in traditional religion. I admit gladly that the Christianity is best in principle than the religion. It is in harmony with principles of growth, while there is very much which is artificial in the selection and arrangement of Scripture and methods, and artificiality always leads to necessary complexity. But the easy and the simple are not identical. To discover what is really simple and to act upon the discovery is not an exceedingly difficult task. After the artificial and complex is once institutionally established and ingrained in custom and routine, it is easier to walk in the Christian paths that have been beaten than it is, after taking a new point of view of life, to work out what is practically involved in the new point of view of life. The religion system was not more complicated with its belief, truth, and faith are often used always does even where there is no evidence or proof. So we come back to the idea that coherent theory of experience, affording positive direction to selection and organization of appropriate Christian methods and materials, is required by the attempt to give new direction to the work of the church. The process is a slow and arduous one. It is a matter of growth, and there are many obstacles which tend to obstruct growth and to deflect it into wrong people. I shall have something to say later about church. All that is needed, perhaps, at this point is to say that we must escape from the tendency to think of churches in terms of the kind of church, whether of content or Religion or Christianity, or of methods and social relations, that mark traditional belief. I think that a good deal of the current opposition to the idea of churches is due to the fact that it is so hard to get away from the picture of the studies of the Old Belief named Religion.

The moment "Religion" is mentioned imagination goes almost automatically to the kind of religion that is familiar, and in revolting against that we are led to shrink from the very idea of any religious organization. On the other hand, educational reactionaries, who are now gathering force, use the absence of adequate intellectual and moral religious in the newer type of church as proof not only of the need of religious organization, but to identify any and every kind of religious with that instituted before the rise of experimental belief. Failure to develop a conception of religious upon the empirical and experimental basis gives reactionaries a too easy victory. But the fact that the empirical beliefs now offer the best type of intellectual religion which can be found in any field shows that there is no reason why we, who call ourselves empiricists, should be pushovers, in the matter of order and religious organization. It may well be asked, in view of all that has been said, in what sense, if any, we can properly speak of the Bible as the Word of God. When the Scriptures were regarded as literally inerrant, the beliefs being passive instruments in God's hands, there was a clear and definite sense in which the Scriptures could be called the Word of God, by both faiths. When the Scriptures were regarded as literally inerrant, the prophet being passive instruments in God's hands, there was a clear and definite sense in which the Scriptures could be called he Word of God. God wrote the Scriptures, and they were therefore his written Word. But when this view is rejected, and we regard it as both a right and a duty to exercise a discriminatory judgment on the Scriptures, the time honored phrase, the Word of God, if we continue to use it, obviously calls for fresh exposition and definition. The need becomes the more evident when inquiry reveals that both in the Bible itself and in theological usage the phase, the Word of God, has had a number of variant though not unrelated meanings. We as Christian belief in the Son of God, Jesus Christ. The Word of God , main meaning kind of religion from the main meaning in Christianity. In the New Testament the concept of the "Word", or variant phrases such as "Word of God" or "Word of the Cross" or "Word of the Gospel", seems to bear the following main meanings: (1) the content of the gospel message, as disclosed to mankind by God through Jesus Christ, and as witnessed to in the preaching of the Gospel. Isaiah 61:1; Luke 19:10; John 3:16,17; Romans 5:8,11; I Cor. 15:55,57; Luke 4:16; Matt. 28:18,20; John 16:13,15; Rev. 1:2; Phil. 2:16. (2) the total truth for life, conduct, and belief, which is implicit in the gospel proclamation, and which must be accepted if the full riches of the gospel are to be enjoyed. Also see Col. 1:5; Tit. 1:9; Pet. 2:8; James 1:22. (3) Jesus Christ activity in salvation, both within the hearts and minds of believers and in the church. Heb. 4:12; 6:5; Eph. 5:26; Col. 3:16; and finally. (4) the Scripture state that God's eternal being in an eternally outgoing activity of creative reason, which creates the world, gives life and understanding to men, and finally becomes incarnate in Jesus Christ. John 1:1, 4; I John. 1:1; Rev. 19:13. As I stated that, we are Christian. It is not difficult to see what is the dominant, and unifying thought of all these usages. The Word of God signifies the revealing activity of the living and personal God in creation and toward men and women, particularly as this is manifest and operative in the gospel, being here used as an all-inclusive term to signify. (a) the content of the gospel, namely, that God himself came in a supreme, saving act of self-giving and self- disclosure in Jesus Christ. (b) the declaration of the gospel through the preaching and teaching of its primary witnesses, and; © the making of the gospel effective in the hearts and lives of those who believe. To this wealth of meaning all of it centering in the thought of the revealing activity of God toward men and women, the symbol of the Word is singularly appropriate; it would be difficult to think of one more compendiously ad equate. However, the course of thought which has been pursued in this book may perhaps be taken to afford sufficient ground for adhering to what has become the Protestant tradition of speaking of the Bible as the Word of God; though it at the same time defines the sense in which we may do so. For we have maintained that the Scriptures do enter indispensable into that revealing and saving activity of God in the incarnate Redeemer and in the gospel message concerning him, which is what the symbol of the Word of God properly denotes. God, as it were, continually takes the Jesus word of the Bible up into his own living Word, so that it becomes vitally one, though not identical, with it. To speak of the Scripture as the Word of God, for all the misrepresentation and misuse to which such a usage is admittedly exposed, does least forbid us to minimize or overlook this vital union and its necessity. Nor, it must be emphasized again, is this indispensable union of the Scriptures with the saving Word of God in Jesus Christ and the Gospel message impaired in the least by the fact that we must use our own best knowledge and judgment to interpret them. On the contrary, our freedom to do this is used by God, in his patience and wisdom, the Word of God into a living encounter with us as persons, whom he must save as persons, if we are to be saved at all conclusion, each of us acts today and hopes for tomorrow in the light of past experiences that have been woven into life story of Religion and Christianity. When we want to know another person, we ask him or her to tell us something of the story of his or her life; for in this was he or she discloses who he or she really is. To be self is to have a personal history. We remember the Religion philosophy. For this reason, we cannot begin to understand the Old Testament, so long as we regard it as merely great literature, interesting history, or the development of lofty ideas. The Old Testament is the narration of

God's action. What they has done, is doing, and will do. All human history is the theater of his or her self-disclosure, and nature too is his or her handiwork; but he or she acts particularly within the career of a comparatively obscure people in order to initiate a historical drama that has changed human perspectives and has altered the course of human affairs. When an individual seeks to understand the meaning of his or her life-story, he or she does not actually begin with the birth of a infancy, even though his written autobiography may start at that point, his name is "Jesus Christ".

CHAPTER 3

The Understand of a Theory of Christianity

If there is any truth in what has been said about the need of forming a theory of Christian experience in order that education may be intelligently conducted upon the basis of experience, it is clear that the next thing in order in this discussion is to present the principles that are most significant in framing this theory. I shall not, therefore , apologize for engaging in a certain amount of philosophical belief which otherwise might be out of place, concern Religion and Christianity. I may, however, reassure you to some degree by saying that this belief is not an end in itself but is engaged in for the sake of obtaining Christian to be applied later in discussion of a number of reality and, to most persons, more interesting issues. I have already mentioned what I called Religion and Christianity. The criteria of Christianity of stated as follows: (1) Atonement: The bringing together of humankind and God through the atonement is the center of gravity in the New Testament, as a mere census of references immediately demonstrates. According to apostolic preaching and doctrine, the significance of Jesus Christ does not lie supremely in his person or ministry or teaching; it ties supremely in his death upon the cross. In the New Testament to be sure, that even is never viewed in isolation from his person, his ministry, and his teaching; nor is it viewed apart from his resurrection. His death exegetes his teaching, and together with his sin-free, miracle-working ministry of love, constitutes the active obedience of life "to use the Calvinistic formulation" without which the passive obedience of suffering would have been nugatory. Yet it is the event of Christ's death which the New Testament consistently underscores as all important, and his death interpreted not as a martyrdom, brought to pass by a miscarriage of justice, but as the offering of a redemptive sacrifice in Hebrews 10:1-14. This event, this saving deed, in the whole range of its results, is commonly called the atonement. (2) Baptism: The sacrament of immersion in water, whereby a person is initiated into the Christian church. On this basis it has been practiced by almost all Christians, it by a baptism of Fire of the Spirit in terms in Matthew 3:11. The Reformers agreed that his best brought out the meaning of baptism as a death and resurrection, but even the early Ana- Baptists did not think it essential so long as the subject goes under the water. The type of water and circumstances of administration are not important, though it seems necessary that there should be a preaching and confession of Jesus Christ as integral parts of the administration in Acts 8:37; Matthew 16:16. Other ceremonies may be used at discretion so long as they are not unscriptural and do not distract from the true action, like the complicated and rather superstitious ceremonial of the medieval and modern Roman Church. Discussion has been raised concerning the proper ministers and subjects of the action. In the first instance there may be agreement with Augustine that Jesus Christ himself is the true minister "he shall baptize you", Matthew 3:11. But Jesus Christ does not give the external baptism directly; he commits this to his disciples in John 4:2 says: "though Jesus himself baptized not, but his disciples". This is taken to mean that baptism should be administered by those to whom there is entrusted by inward and outward calling the ministry of word and sacrament, though laymen have been allowed baptize though laymen have been allowed to baptize in the Roman Church at "Lay Baptism", and some early Baptists conceived the strange notion of baptizing themselves. Like all preaching, however, baptism carries with it the call to that which we should do in response or correspondence to what Jesus Christ has done for us. We, too, must make our movement of death and resurrection, not to add to what Jesus Christ has done, nor to complete it, nor to compete with it, but in grateful acceptance and application. We do this in three related ways constantly kept before us by our baptism. The essentials are that we use it. (a) to present Jesus

Christ; (b) in prayer to the Holy Spirit; (c) in trustful dependence upon his sovereign work, and; (d) in conjunction with the spoken word. Restored to this evangelical use, and freed especially from distorting and unhelpful controversy, baptism might quickly manifest again its power as a summons to live increasingly or even to begin to live, the life which is our in Jesus Christ crucified and risen for us. (3) Bible: The collection of books which are treated by Christians as the record of God's revelation. The word Bible as we use it today, however, has a far more significant connotation than the Greek meaning. While biblical was somewhat natural, it could be used to designate books of magic in Acts 19:19 or a bill of divorcement in Mark 10:4 as well as sacred books, the word Bible refers to the Book, the recognized record of divine revelation. Although this meaning is ecclesiastical in origin, its roots go back into the Old Testament. This usage passed into the Christian church. The process by which the various books in the Bible were brought together and their value as sacred Scripture recognized is referred to as the history of the canon. The Bible incorporates much oral material which was repeated from father to son in very ancient days, reworked time and again, then put into written form by various editors and redactors. The Hebrew Old Testament divided its 24 books as below. I and II Samuel; I and II Kings; I and II Chronicles; Ezra and Nehemiah. "The Twelve" Minor Prophets were counted as one book. Note also the order, differing from the Old Testament, of Christian usage.

The Law

Genesis, Exodus, Leviticus, Numbers, and Deuteronomy

The Prophets

"The former Prophets", Joshua, Judges, Samuel, and Kings.

"The Latter Prophets": Isaiah, Jeremiah, Ezekiel.

"The Twelve" Minor Prophets: Hosea, Joel, Amos, Obadiah, Jonah, Micah, Nahum, Habakkuk, Zephaniah, Haggai, Zechariah, and Malachi.

The Writings

Psalms, Proverbs, Job, Ruth, Song of Solomon, Lamentations, Ecclesiastes, Esther, Daniel, Ezra, Nehemiah, and Chronicles.

Three language were used in the original Bible Hebrew, for most of the Old Testament with a few Aramaic passages. Greek for the New Testament, with Aram based material incorporated. The trilingual super Scripture above the head of the crucified Saviour included one line in Latin in Luke 23: 38. Today the Bible, in part or entirety, has been published in more than 1,151 languages, as reported by the American Bible Society, 1960. The Bible that Christian used in the King James Version Bible contains 773,692 words. (4) Jesus Christ: The anointed one or Messiah who is the agent of salvation. The given name of God's incarnate Son, given before by divine intimation in Matt. 1: 21; Luke 1:31, and then in due course by parental bestowment in Luke 2:21. Jesus is the Greek form of Jeshua or Joshua in Acts 7:45; Heb. 4:8, meaning the Lord is salvation or the salvation of the Lord. The name has affinity with that of the great evangelical prophet Isaiah, whose predictions give prominence to the Messiah under various titles. Most important of all, the name was a reminder of the character and purpose of Israel's God as delighting in the salvation of his people. The historic deliverances of the past "Exodus and Restoration from Babylon", serving to underscore his pledge of messianic salvation for the future. Reflection on the meaning of his name must have been a constant reminder to Jesus of his mission; in the world as it probably was to his church in I Thess. 1:10. From any point of view, Jesus Christ is the central figure of the Bible. Hosea, Jeremiah, and the Second Isaiah may fairly be said to stand by themselves in the Old Testament, but he is the blossom of which they were the bud. The prophets proclaimed the word of God as they were given to see it, but at last it was said of Jesus Christ that he was "the Word made Flesh", in John 1:14. (5) Church: The existence of the church is a revelation of the gracious heart of God. The Father chose his eternal Son to become the Saviour of sinners, the Messiah of the whole Israel of God. In him God chose the people for his own possession and called individuals into this fellowship. This the people of God includes the patriarchs, the congregation of ancient Israel, Jesus and his disciples, the primitive community of his resurrection, and the Christian church. For the people of God, the Old Testament period was the dispensation of promise, the New Testament that of fulfillment. Jesus Christ revealed not a new God, but a new way of worshiping the same God. In the Old Testament it is the whole assembly of the congregation of Israel in Deut.

31:30, who hear the law. Remember, Jesus Christ brings and keeps his disciple and his people in covenant fellowship with himself by his Spirit and his word in Isaiah. 59: 21. His voice is heard in the proclamation of his Word and his acts are seen in the administration of his sacraments. Accordingly, these with prayer and praise are the marks of the visible church, the means the Holy Spirit uses to bring individuals to personal faith and to nourish believers in the corporate worship of the Christian community. As we receive God's promises, He forgives the sins of his people and seals us with his sacraments for the world to come mean the present, and future. As to the former, the church is a fact established by God. It is His supernatural act. According to the consentient testimony of the Old and of the New Testaments, this is not a man made myth but a God given fact. The same God who spoke the word of promise to ancient Israel speak the word of fulfillment to the Christian church. As the Father reveals the Son, the Messiah builds his church in Matt.16:17-18; 11:25-30. At Pentecost the three miracles manifest the direct action of God establishing his church. The New Testament speaks of the church as God building, his planting, his vineyard, his temple, his household, his olive tree, his city and his people. God's acts in the church are in Jesus Christ. An adequate recognition of Jesus Christ as the Messiah and of the mighty acts of God in him establishes the integral relation of the church to her Lord. The King Messiah and the disciple, and people of God belong together. We are like, the shepherd implies the flock, as the hen gathers her chickens under her wings, as the vine has many branches, the body its several members, as the foundation supports its building, as the Servant justifies many, as the Son of Man stands for the saints of the Most High, as the King implies the kingdom, so the Messiah has his twelve and Jesus Christ his church. Jesus Christ spoke of "My Church" and of "My Flock", and these two are linked together in Acts. 20:28. We are the heavenly church the bride awaiting on Jesus Christ her Bridegroom in Mark 2:19-20; II Cor. 11:2; Romans 7:1-6. Jesus Christ loved the church and gave himself up for her. Having cleansed the church by the washing of water with the Word, he is now sanctifying her in order that he may present her spotless for the marriage feast of the Lamb.

(6) Communion: The communion of saints is the second clause of the ninth article of the Apostles Creed, traceable to the text of Nicety

as of Aquilegia in the fifth century, is probably the latest addition to the Roman symbol, but is of uncertain origin and implication. Known also as the Eucharist in Anglicanism, the mass in Roman Catholicism, and the liturgy in Eastern Orthodoxy; the primary sacrament of sharing Christ's life by partaking of the bread and wine as his body and blood. (7) Grace: The power of God entering into humans to empower them to good deeds and salvation. The essence of the doctrine of grace is that God is for us. What is more, he is for us who in ourselves are against him. Most still, he is not for us merely in a general attitude, but has effectively acts towards us. Grace is summed up in the name Jesus Christ. Jesus Christ is God for us. We may consider this in terms of the covenant. In the Son of God binds himself freely to us to be our God, and binds us to himself to be his. By becoming our God he becomes to us what he is in himself, loving, holy, merciful, and patient, in a word, gracious. As he is God in himself, so he will be God toward us, for our benefit. He will assume the responsibility for our past, present, and future. He no longer an enemy, stands with us against our real enemies, and that effectively. "If God be for us, who can be against us?", in Romans 8:31. But all this is true because Jesus Christ has come, died and risen again. "For the law was given by Moses, but grace and truth cam by Jesus Christ", in John 1: 17. Because grace is God's free decision upon us in Jesus Christ, proceeding from his graciousness, it follows that we have no ability to win his grace or favor. This is why grace is opposed to the works of the law tacitly throughout the New Testament and expressly in such passages as in Romans 3:19; John 1:17; Gal. 2:11-21;Eph. 2:8-9. On the contrary, grace must be acknowledged for what it is and accepted with humble and joyful gratitude. This human decision, involving acknowledgement and acceptance, is the faith which corresponds to God's grace. "By grace are ye saved through faith; and that not of yourselves : it is the gift of God". In Eph. 2:8. (8) Ikon: A picture used in Orthodoxy as a window on heaven, and an object of devotion to the faithful. (9) Love: Greek agape, the reverential affection for other human beings which is the primary Christian virtue. Scripture defines love in the only way that it can or ought to be defined; namely, by listing its attributes. Remember, love is patient and kind, love is not jealous or boastful; it is not arrogant or rude. Love does not insist on its own way; it is not irritable or resentful; it does not rejoice at wrong, but rejoices in the right. Love bears all things, believes all things, hopes all things, endures all things in I Cor. 13:7. Love is fellowship between persons; it is an act of self surrender. Also, God is love in His very essence in John 4:8-16. The eternal, self-generating nature of God actuates itself in mutual self-surrender between Father, Son, and Holy Spirit. When Jesus Christ came to earth, he incarnated perfect love. He bore the very stamp of the divine nature; those who saw him saw the Father. Ever Christ's enemies could find no fault in him. Salvation was conceived by the love of God. The Father planned salvation; the Son executed it; and the Holy Spirit applies it. There is such perfect unity in the Godhead that some acts of redemption are attributed to either a specific person or to the God-head essentially. The resurrection of Jesus Christ is an example of this. Love is the true point of contact between God and mankind. Mankind is made in the image of God, and the image of God is the capacity of self-surrender. The more kind and loving a man or woman is, the most like God he or she is. A good man or woman prefers others before himself or herself; a bad man or woman is selfish. Therefore, when Christians are commanded to love, the command is a much a judgment against unloveliness as it is a pre-scripture to be lovely. The first of all the commandments is, Hear O Israel; The Lord our God is one Lord: And thou shalt love the Lord thy God with all thy heart, and with all thy soul, and with all thy mind and with all thy strength". Mark 12:29-30. Since we are totally dependent upon God, we are not rightly related to God unless we are totally surrendered. Love for God issues in worship, and worship issues in fellowship, a fellowship made possible by the life and death of Jesus Christ. The second greatest commandment is like, namely, this. "Thou shalt love thy neighbour as thyself", in Mark 12:31. Every normal human being has a sense of his or her own spiritual dignity written on his or her heart. We are to love our neighbor with the same degree of zeal and consistency with which we love ourselves. And since there is no practical limit to the claims of self love, there is no practical limit to our duty toward a neighbor. Love is the mark of a true Christian. " By this all men will know that you are my disciples, if you have love for one another" in John 13:35. (10) Sin: The estrangement of humans from God, thought to be due to the actions of Adam and Eve in the first instance. The biblical revelation concerning the nature of sin lies embedded in sacred history. In Genesis 3, the origin of sin in the human race is attributed to the fall of Adam and Eve in Eden. From the Bible the following truths are established. (a) that God is not the author of sin, but that sin is suggestively, then overtly proposed by the serpent and freely embraced by Eve. (b) that the sin of Eve begins with doubt concerning the rightness of God's command not to eat of the fruit of the tree of the knowledge of good and evil. © that the sinful act resulting from rationalized desire was one of direct and willful disobedience to the expressed command of God. (d) that the first sinful act by both Adam and Eve resulted in an immediate sense of the shamefulness of nakedness and a consequent attempt to hide from God; and people are doing the same things today. (e) that the sin is followed by the divine curse on the serpent, as (Satan) who beguiled woman, and man and expulsion from fellowship with God in the garden. The penalty of death is inflicted on the human race which descends from Adam and Eve in Gen. 3:4-6. Because of sin, mankind corrupts its way upon the earth and its extreme wickedness evokes the judgment of the floor in Gen. 6. The New Testament contains in which sin is defined or described in broad terms. Jesus Christ says, "Whosoever committeth sin is the servant of sin", in Romans 6:16-20-23; II Peter 2:19. The Gospels presuppose and hardly define the sinfulness of men and women. But the Old Testament conception of sin as rebellion against covenant grace takes on new form. Jesus says, "for I am not come to call the righteous, but sinners to repentance" in Matt. 9:13; I Tim. 1: 15. The power of sin is awakened by the law and the observation of sin's reaction to law leads Paul to confess, "For we know that the law is spiritual: but I am carnal, sold under sin", Romans 7:14. Sin consists not simply in deeds but in a condition, a condition common to all men and women who are by nature dead in trespasses and sins and are children of wrath. Paul says, "And you hath he quickened, who were dead in trespasses and sins" in Eph. 2:1. Apart from Jesus Christ mankind is in the flesh and from this source come all kinds of actual sins, in Galatians 5:19. Sin is essentially a religious idea, it always presupposes God and his law; this is why the conception of God determines what is regarded as sinful. Always in the Bible teaching sin has a God reference. Men or women are sinner because they have gone contrary to the will of God, or to what they took his or her will to be, or to what they might have known his or her will to be. This rebelliousness is charged to all. "There is none righteous, no not one" in Romans 3: 10. As you know that sin, however, goes deeper than the will, it is primarily a matter of the heart. The sinful deed expresses a still deeper sinfulness, and the problem lies with that deeper sinfulness, that is, with the natural disposition. This accounts for the Biblical stress on the clean heart. This is in the Bible, however, the recognition not only of individual sin but of corporate or general sin as well. Corporate sin presupposes such an intimate relationship among the members of a group that the sin of one becomes the sin of all. Adam's sin becomes the sin of all his posterity; the sin of Achan made all his family guilty in Josh. 7. The Bible sets the reign of love over against the reign of sin, and sees Jesus Christ as God's supreme means for creating love. (11) Thesis: Profess of becoming divinized or like God; the goal of Easter Orthodox spiritual effort. (12) Trinity: God as three in one, as Father, Son and Holy Spirit; being three persons or centers of consciousness in one being. It signifies that within the one essence of the Godhead we have to distinguish three 'persons" who are neither three gods on the one side, not three parts or modes of God on the other, but coequally and coeternally God. In the Trinity as properly understood no such independence is possible; all three Persons must exist in order for any one of the Persons to exist. Because God's existence as a Trinity is as necessary as his mere existence. God does not choose to exist, and he could not choose not to exist. He does not choose the manner of his existence, nor could he change the manner. He must be what he is and how he is. None of the three Persons can exist or act save in relation to the other two. The manner of God's existence as triune is not the result of mutual agreement, and it could not be changed by agreement. The Father must be the Father, the Son must be the Son; The Holy Spirit must be the Holy Spirit; and God must be such a threefold being as this involves. It is true that Christianity speaks of the Father as the First Person, and of the Son as the Second Person, and of the Holy Spirit as the Third Person; but "first" or "second" and "third" here do not represent a time order rather the order of necessary relationships. It is of the nature of the Son to depend on the Father, and it is the nature of the Holy Spirit to depend on the Father and Son.

CHAPTER 4

The Meaning of Purpose

It is, then, a sound instinct which identifies freedom with power to frame purposes and to execute or carry into effect purposes so framed. Such freedom is in turn identical with self-control, for the formation of purposes and the organization of means to execute them are the work of intelligence. As I wrote in Chapter 1 page 3, stated that Christianity matter, which will be discussed in some detail later. The problem we are facing that we have to differ beliefs. (1) Religion (2) Christianity. Religion is a belief. Study may best be thought of as a system embodying the means of attaining and expressing in conduct the values deemed characteristic of the ideal life, including concepts of belief in sacred rites, sacrifices, and offering. Example, Hebrew and Christian though religion is mankind recognition of his or her relation to God and his or her expression of that relation in faith, worship, and conduct. Christianity is the based on the teachings of Jesus Christ and His Apostles. Between the 2d century the first used of the world Christian letters of Ignatius, Bishop of Antioch. It is a revelation of God through His Son Jesus Christ; a way of life based on a personal experience of Jesus Christ. Though the term Christian appears three times in the New Testament, the time was not yet ripe for its companion word, which came into use in the second century as a designation for the belief which centers in Jesus Christ. Before Judaic Christian dwindled into comparative insignificance, it passed on its heritage to the Gentiles, who were reached through Greek-speaking Jews, such Barnabas and Paul. It is also supernatural in character, for it frankly depends upon revelation. Men and women is no longer feeling out after God but is resting on the divine self-disclosure in Christ. God has become incarnate in his Son, who confirmed the revelation in the Old Testament and added to it by his teaching and by personal impact. To see him was to see the Father. The miraculous element in Christianity is agreeably to its supernatural nature. History ceases to the riddle. Eternity has dipped into time divine nature has taken human form in order to reveal itself fully and to life man into fellowship with God. Christianity is Trinity, acknowledging God the Father, Son, and Holy Spirit. In this it is distinguished from the other belief that there is only one God. The Christian faith is also exclusive. It does not grant that men and women are saved by any other means than the Gospel of Jesus Christ. It deriver this conviction from the teaching of Scripture, and not from partisan feeling or narrowness of out look. It does not deny good in other beliefs, nor does it claim to have all truth . Rather, it rejoices in the truth which God has been pleased to reveal, which is sufficient for salvation. Exclusivism only becomes offensive when it ceases to be missionary. Christianity may be viewed as a creed, but behind its confession is a personal relation to the Saviour. It may very from place to place in its form of government, but it everywhere acknowledges the lordship of Jesus Christ. Its forms of worship may differ from church to church, but its aim is to glorify God and to make known his saving grace. Remember, creed are statements of our basic belief about God. Some churches use two or three creeds. Christianity is this faith, with its influence on our livers, thoughts and actions. Because what we are, and the purpose for which we live depend on our beliefs. Some Politicians are Christian but they belief in science. Because what we are, and the purpose what we live depend on our beliefs. Some say, that science can explain all things and that Christianity is not necessary. This is not true, science can explain many things, but there are other which are of the highest importance for which science cannot give the answers. Science cannot explain love, good and evil, the freedom of all peoples will, art music, the purpose for which we live, what happens after death or why and how the universe was created. Science knows nothing of God and man's soul. In short, most of the things which give our lives meaning and distinguish us from the animals are outside the realm of science. Some believe that science and Christianity contradictory. No, they deal with reality and truth in different ways. But are important and necessary, and they complement each other. Science seek to explain a part of reality, the visible or measurable world, and to attain truth in physical world through the use of people's senses and there reasons. It has great importance and value for mankind. Christian seek to find the meaning of this world and the place and purpose of man and woman life in it. It deals with ethics, with man and woman relation to man and woman and the world, and with what happens after death. It seek to know God and his relation to man and woman and to find out what his will for man and woman is. Christianity teaches us that we can come to know God through God's revelation of himself in his creation in the Bible, and supremely in Jesus Christ. Although we are human beings with our finite minds, cannot be God or his existence, belief in God enable us to understand many things which would otherwise be inexplicable, such as the universe came to be for what purpose, without belief in God we are mere human in a mechanistic universe, without freedom meaning of purpose, and our end is unremembered seat in the face of blind forces leading to ultimate chaos. But belief in God, as Christianity understands it, is not merely assent to an abstract hypothesis, but a living, personal relationship of love with the author of our being. How do we know that is the true? We can not prove it, and we can only find out by living it. However, there are a number of things about Christianity which ought to make us consider it. Christianity is the largest faith in the United States and it grow in the world and the most international with almost than $100,000,000,000 or more believers. It is the true Christian of many of the most advanced nations, and is the faith held by many of the world's greatest thinkers and philosophy both now and in the past. Even though it has been attacked and persecuted, for almost 3,001 years, the Christian faith has been held fast by men and women who were ready to die for it in all nations, and the faith is still growing today. These are not proofs, but they indicate that Christianity, more than any other faith, should be taken seriously and studied carefully by all. Although the truth is one, men and women see it from different angles. As we draw nearer the truth, our beliefs will also grow closer together. Although there are many denominations in Christianity because of our imperfections and inadequate understanding our faith is one in most important fundamentals. We worship God's believe in the Saviour Jesus Christ, and read the Bible. We try to cooperate with each other and are working and praying greater unity. We can know something of God through our reason and through seeing the things which he has made, including man. Through our consciences and through the testimony of others, particularly in the church, we can learn more. But most of all we can come to know God through the Bible. There are glimpses of God's truth in other belief and their writings, in the works of religious, philosophers and poets and scientists outside Christianity. But only in the Bible can we find the true nature of God revealed clearly. It is our primary source of revelation. In it God reveals himself to man. It is important that peoples maintain an interest in the Bible. The Bible teach us to respect others as yourself and understanding there habits. Because we are Christian and have this great distinction and dignity of the Christianity. We are free and have rights and duties, make senses to us, all although they not even to so superior an good and evil. We are responsible before God and our fellow man and woman and our souls. We deserve respect from ourselves and from all men and women, no matter how dab or how sinful or ignorant a person me be. We deserve respect from all, they deserve respect too. Act 10:34 reads, "Then Peter opened his mouth, and said, Of a truth I perceive that God is no respecter of persons". This is true, simply because of our noble distinction as Christians. Romans 2:11 reads, "For there is no respect of persons with God". Wrote, " Philosophers have always been impressed by the wonderful attributes of the human being. They have said that we are more like God than are all other living and non-living things are around us" , I see that and commanded to honor and respect the person in himself and herself. This command has a broad base. It is "Love, Respect, Understanding, and Forgive". It is find in Jesus Christ, while not accepting persons showed that respect must be given where it is due. If you reader James 2:1-9, it is well illustrates the meaning of the term in Christian conduct. If anyone is dishonoring and disrespecting the person, in himself or herself or anyone else, he or she is to some extent canceling out his own being. We have noted that unsocial behavior is any behavior denying someone else the respect that everyone owes himself or herself. The fundamental social law of human existence is respect others as yourself. Romans 2:14 reads, "For when the Gentiles, which have not the law, do by nature the things contained in the law, these, having not the law, are a law unto themselves". It is an obvious self-deception when two person try to escape this law by agreeing to renounce self-respect and each thus to rid also of the duty of respecting the other, man's fundamental law urged upon him by the reality of his existence in its social dimension is then; respect everyone else as you should respect yourself. Because man or woman is a person, he or she has the rights of a man or woman rights of being defined as a moral power to do, possess, or demand something. That is basis of his or her most important rights such as the right to life, freedom of conscience and belief, privacy, and the making of certain important decisions for himself or herself. Christianity teach, young people they can learn the lesson of deprivation, and they ought to learn to respect ignorant and unmannerly people and lazy beggars and all the under privileged. This learning has to be included if we really believe in respect for the persons. Christianity teach, they ought to respect there parent, adult, teacher and other peoples; which we cannot do unless we was taught from our childhood. The Sixth Commandment said, "Honor your Father and Mother, that your days may be long in the land which the Lord your God gives you". Some people get into the bad habit of making even of the unfortunate, speaking of them or to them with scorn, and entire families may have the evil habit or not, despising certain persons and groups. On this matter, everyone should frequently examine his or her conscience. It is a grave evil to make fun of and hurt anyone's feelings; if we ever do so, we ought to find ways try to compensate. This is under Deuteronomic Code. Hurting the feelings of persons can be a sin against justice, since we owe to them a fundamental respect. Furthermore, it is wrong to disrespect ever the other race of peoples. Together with the spirit they go to make up the being of persons, so that we cannot violate the body without violating the body without violating the person; include Rape, and other crime offense. Of course, we do not honor gangsters, but gangsters are peoples too, and we honor them as such at the same moment that we dislike the evil in them or in anyone else. We can honor the person and dislike the evil they one does, because the love of Jesus Christ is inside of us. Christianity teach us to love others. Remember, love is patient and kind, love is not jealous or boastful, it is not arrogant or rude. Love does not insist on its own way; it is not irritable or resentful, it does not rejoice at wrong, but rejoices in the right. Love bears all things, believes all things, hope all things, endures all things. Therefore, when Christians are commandment to love, the command is as much a judgment against unloveliness as it is a prescription to be lovely. The key to Christianity is "Love", John 3:16 reads, "For God so loved the world, that he gave his begotten Son, that whosoever believeth in him should not perish, but have everlasting life". Love is the true point of contact between God and man and woman. Man is made in the image of God, and the image of God is the capacity of self-surrender. The more kind and loving a man or woman is, the more like God them. A good man or woman prefers others before himself or herself; a bad man or a bad woman is selfish. Can a young persons be totally responsible for his or her behavior, since he or she may obtain some behavior from tradition, society, and environments. So far as he she knowingly and freely does any good act, he or she deserves credit for it, and so far as he or she does good acts knowing that they lead toward good behavior, he or she deserves credit. Of course, when he or she knowingly and freely does evil acts, they is responsible for them, too, and if they does evil acts knowing that they can lead, as if by a chain reaction, to ward evil behavior, they is responsible for the evil behavior and their effects. A child can respectably do evil acts, that are objective evil, without knowing that they are evil, and if they goes on doing them, through no fault of his or her own; they fall into evil behavior, even though subjectively he or she does no evil. This behavior may go so far, still without responsibility on his or her part; that by the time they discovers that he or she has been evil, and has firmed an evil acts, it may be extremely difficulty, perhaps impossible, for them to break the behavior. This is how seriously, and to what depth, a behavior can modify freedom of action. The young person whole life has been modified toward evil, through fault of themselves. We can kind and thoughtful to a person, even though we may dislike him. Christ commands us to love even our enemies. Matthew 5:45 reads, "That ye may be the children of your Father which is in heaven: for he maketh his sun to rise on the evil and on the good, and sendeth rain on the just and on the unjust". It depends on whether they could be expected to know that had behavior have consequently, more than good would follow. Only the most [Obdurate] and [Rigorist], would hold that a person, knowing doing an evil act, is surely responsible for the possible year and years of evil acts and behavior that may follow in there own life and lives of others.

CHAPTER 5

Understand the Meaning of Religion

In the beginning was the Word, and the Word was God. The same was in the beginning with God. All things were made by him; and without him was made nothing that was made. In him was life, and the life of men, and the Word was made flesh, and dwelt among us, and we saw His glory, the glory as it were of the only begotten of the Father, full of grace and truth. So does St. John Gospel describe the Second Person of the Holy Trinity and His incarnation in the person of Jesus Christ. The doctrine of the Word of God which is at the same time His wisdom and His reason is, of course, not peculiar to Christianity. What makes Christianity unique is not the doctrine of the Eternal Word but the incarnation of what Word in a human being. Jesus Christ too has its doctrine of the Word of God and of the irruption of that Word into the temporal and created world. But whereas in Christianity the Word becomes incarnate in the person of Jesus Christ so that Christ, is the "Gospel", and the Word of God through the volume of the book; is by right and nature the prime object of devotion to the Christian, in Jesus Christ the eternal Word breaks into time not as the Prophet of other Religious, but as the belief which, for their god, is the eternal and consubstantial Word of God. The Prophet of other Religious is merely the vehicle through which the Word is transmitted to man. If, then, the Christians believe in the Word made flesh, the Prophet of Religious believe equally in the Word made Book. We must now consider whether the Religious had such doctrine, and, if so, what they believed the word to be in this material and temporal world. We have already seen that omniscience and goodness make up the permanent disposition of belief and that these were also called "Religion". The interpretation of both is the same, namely the permanent disposition of infinite time, for Belief and the Space, Religion, and Time of other Religions were and are evermore shall be. Thus God's omniscience which is identified with the "Religion", that is the other religion, seems to be the other religious version of the doctrine of the Logos or Word. This religion is itself the very wisdom of God, his thought through which he creates. Thus in the book of Menok I Khrat of "Spirit of Wisdom", we find Wisdom saying. From the first among spiritual and material beings was I who am innate wisdom with other religion. And the creator religion fashioned and created, maintains and orders all spiritual and material creatures, the gods and all the rest of creation through the power and valour, wisdom and experience of innate wisdom. All knowledge and experience on earth, education, and the learning of all trades, and every occupation practiced by men and women in this temporal world, are by wisdom. The souls of the blessed escape from Hell and go to Heaven chiefly through the power and protection of wisdom. And men on earth should seek a good life and happiness and a good name and all good things through the power of wisdom. Similarly it is through wisdom that the embryo is safely preserved in the womb, that the plants grow and the world is full of good things, that the Sun, Mood, and Stars follow their appointed courses, that the rains rain, and finally that man recognizes the truth of the theory of Religion. Wisdom, then is God's Word which gives the world its being and which maintains it in existence; and this Word is identical with the Den, the Religion. As the creative Word of God the Religion is summed up in the prayer book, which, as we have seen, other religion pronounces at the very beginning of creation and which has effect of precipitating Ahriman back into his own kingdom of darkness for three thousand years. By pronouncing his Eternal Word God reveals to his enemy his final defeat and destruction, the creation of the world and its final rehabilitation at the end of time. Ahriman pronouncement of the Ahunvar is the first manifestation of the godhead; it sets the whole creative process in motion and marks the beginning of finite time. Creation, indeed, is the manifestation of God's eternal

Wisdom in the Religion and of his temporal infinity beyond finite time. Is like a mighty tree, with one trunk , two great boughs three branches, for off-branches, and five roots. And the one trunk is the mean, the two great boughs are action and abstention , the three braches are humat, hukht, and huvarsht, that is good thoughts, good words, and good deeds. The four off-branches are the four religious castes by which the Religion and secular life are both maintained, the priesthood, the warrior caste, the caste of husbandmen, and the caste of artisans. Remember, the five roots are the five degrees of government whose names in Religion are "manpat" (householder), "vispat" (village headman), "zandpat" (tribal chieftain), "dehpat" (provincial governor), and the "Zarathrushtotom"(the highest religious authority and representtative of Zoroaster on earth). Over and above these, is another, the Chief of all chiefs, that is the King of Kings, the governor of the whole world. False religion is ruinous heresy; and the forms and vices of ruinous heresy are of the same vile stock as ruinous heresy itself. These forms and vices of ruinous heresy and misbegotten of Akoman, the Evil Mine, and the Destructive Spirit. For the original seed of the theory of Religion is the bounteous spirit, and the original seed of false religion is the destructive spirit. The theory of Religion is manifested in wisdom, conformity with wisdom, in that which has wisdom for its matter and wisdom for its form, in wise action, in good progress that conforms to wisdom, in light which is analogous to wisdom, and in all the benefit that accrues to the good creations is virtue of its being begotten of the bounteous spirit. Remember, false religion is manifested in heresy, conformity with heresy, in that which has heresy for its matter and heresy for its form, in heretical, self-opinionated, action in evil progress that conforms to heresy, in darkness which is analogous to heresy, and in the universal harm that accrues to the good creations in virtue of its being misbegotten of the Destructive Spirit. In the mixed state, the sphere of influence of both belief is in the material world in which innate wisdom and ruinous heresy struggle for supremacy . In the mixed state the degree in which innate wisdom is strong and sovereign corresponds exactly to the degree in which the Religion is accepted , believed, and propagated, the gods reign, the good is great, and the temporal world prospers. So too, the degree in which ruinous heresy is strong and great corresponds exactly to the degree in which false religion is accepted and spread abroad, the demons hold violent way, evil men and women are great, and the temporal world declines. Now we must speak of the belief of these influences. The belief of the Religion is the benefit of creatures, that of false religion is their harm. The belief of the benefit "brought" by the religion whose sphere of influence in the pure state is among the Ahriman, consists in the protection, extended by them to creatures against the disruption caused by the aggressor, the emanation of the power of their goodness into human nature by guarding the will in purity, by disciplining, the character, by establishing in man his very humanity which is his salvation and his adornment, by increasing and multiplying virtue in the world, and by ordering the world in goodness. The beliefs and benefits of the Religion, whose sphere of influence in the mixed state is in man and woman consist in the strengthening of good character and of the virtues in man and woman, in the overcoming and conquest of the lie, in the sanctification of man and woman actions so that his or her soul may be saved, in its total diffusion throughout the human race, the defeat of the host of the lie, the destruction, and expulsion of the aggressor from creation, and the gift of immortality and sovereignty in freedom to all the good creation. The belief of the harm of false religion whose evil sphere of influence in the pure state is among the demons, consists in their pouring out adversity in order to destroy the material world and to damage creatures. And the belief of the harm of false religion, whose sphere of influence in the mixed state is in man and woman, consists in the strengthening of the vices and weakening of the virtues; in the destruction of man and woman very humanity and in sowing devilry in him or her, in the vitiating of his or her actions and the damnation of his or her soul; in doing damage to the earth and in laying it waste by injustice through the corruption of man and woman's humanity by devilry. Injustice gives strength to the demons in their ruining of the material world. Were evil allowed to run its course, unmixed and wholly unrestrained, and were goodness to be annihilated in the world, completely, it would mean that creation, in such a state of total evil unmixed with goodness, could not exist or endure even for a moment. The original word of the Religion is that all good comes from the Creator and that no evil comes from him: in this is contained all the good that creatures enjoy from the original creation till the final Rehabilitation. Thou from belief in this original word of

41

the Religion proceeds the formation of character, from the formation of character the mean: from the mean is justice born, from justice good thoughts, good works, and good deeds; from good thoughts, good words, and good deeds the welfare of man and woman. By the welfare of man and woman are the gods well pleased and strengthened and the demons distressed and vanquished. When the gods are well pleased and strengthened and the demons distressed and vanquished, the spiritual world is made straight and the material world brought into order. When the spiritual world is thus made straight and the material world put in order, creation is ripe for the final Rehabilitation and merges into it, the Rehabilitation is brought about and all creation is administered in purity and goodness. The original word of false religion is that evil comes from the Creator; in this is contained all the evil that creatures suffer from the original creation till the final Rehabilitation. Thus from being beguiled by this original word of false religion proceeds the corruption of character, from corruption of character excess and deficiency, from excess and deficiency injustice, from injustice, evil thoughts, evil words, and evil deeds, and from evil thoughts, evil words, and evil deeds, the distress of man and woman. By the distress of man and woman are the demons rejoiced and the gods distressed. When the demons are rejoiced and the gods distressed, then are the demons emboldened to upset and disturb the temporal world and to do harm and injury to the material world. The Religion and Christianity reveals that these two dignities will meet together around the Kingdom of Heaven. We who are Christian, who believe in Jesus Christ will hear the voice of God says: "Behold, I come quickly: blessed is he that keepeth the sayings of the prophecy of this book". And, behold, I come quickly; and my reward is with me, to give every man according as his work shall be. I am Alpha and Omega, the beginning and the end, the first and the last. As a Christian, I understand John as he wrote in Revelation 21:7 reads, "He that overcometh shall inherit all things; and I will be his God, and he shall be my son"; and John continual to write is Rev. 22:11 reads, "He that is unjust, let him be unjust still: and he which is filthy, let him be filthy still: and he that is righteous, let him be righteous still: and he that is holy, let him be holy still". Rev.22:14 reads, "Blessed are they that do his commandments, that they may have right to the tree of life, and may enter in through the gates into the city".

All Religious has faith and belief in God. Remember, faith is the state of being ultimately concerned; the dynamics of faith are the dynamics of man or woman ultimate concern. Man or woman, like every living being, is concerned about many things, above all about those which condition his or her very existence, such as food and shelter. But man or woman, in contrast to other belief, has spiritual concerns cognitive, aesthetic, social, political. Some of them are urgent, often extremely urgent, and each of them as well as the vital concerns can claim ultimacy for a human life or the life of a social group.

CHAPTER 6

The Understand the Criteria of Economic

If there is any truth in what has been said about the need of forming a theory of economy in order that Christian people may be intelligently conducted upon the basis of economic, it is clear that the next thing in order in this discussion is to present the principles that are most significant in framing this theory. I shall not, therefore, apologize for engaging in a certain amount of biblical analysis, which otherwise might be out of place or not. I may, however, reassure you to some degree by saying that this analysis is not an end in itself but is engaged in for the sake of obtaining to be applied later in discussion of a number of concrete and, to most persons, more interesting issues. I have already mentioned what I called the category of continuity, or the economic continuum. This principle is involved, as I pointed out, in every attempt to discriminate between Religion that are worth while Christianity and those that are not. It may seem superfluous to argue that this discrimination is necessary not only in criticizing the traditional type of economy but also in initiating and conducting a different type. Nevertheless, it is advisable to pursue for a little while the idea that it is necessary. One may safely assume, I suppose, that one thing which has recommended the progressive economic is that it seems more in accord with the democratic ideal to which the Christian is committed than do the procedures of the old traditional Christian, since the latter have so much of the autocratic about them. Another thing which has contributed to its favorable reception is that its methods are humane in comparison with the harshness so often attending the policies or by-law or constitution or canon of the traditional Christian. The question I would raise concerns why are prefer churches and humane arrangements to those which are auto-critic and harsh. And this is, why, I mean the reason for preferring them, not just the economic which lead us to the preference. One economy may be that we have been taught not only in the churches but by the press, the pulpit, the platform, and our policies or by-law or constitution or canon , and law-making bodies that Christian is the best of all social institutions. We may have so assimilated this idea from our surroundings that it has become an habitual part of our mental and moral makeup. But similar causes have led Religion organization in different surroundings to widely varying conclusions, to prefer fascism, for example. The cause for our preference is not the same thing as the reason why we should prefer it. It is not my purpose here to go in detail into the reason. But I would ask a question, can we find any reason that does not ultimately come down to the belief that Christian social arrangements promote a better quality of human experience, one which is more widely accessible and enjoyed, than do non-Christian forms of social life? Does not the principle of regard for individual freedom and for decency and kindliness of human relations come back in the end to the conviction that these things are tributary to a higher quality of economic on the part of a greater number than are methods of repression and coercion or force? It not the church for our preference that we believe that mutual consultation and convictions reached through persuasion, make possible a better quality of experience than can otherwise be provided on any wide scale? If the answer to these questions is in the affirmative, and personally I do not see how can justify our preference for the church and humanity on any other ground, the ultimate reason for hospitality to progressive economic, because of its reliance upon and use of humane methods and its kinship to Christian, goes back to the fact that discrimination is made between the inherent values of different economic. So I come back to the principle of as a criterion of economic. At bottom, this principle rests upon the fact of habit, when habit is interpreted biologically. The basic characteristic of habit is that every economic enacted and undergone modifies the one who acts and undergoes, while this modification affects, whether we wish it or not, the quality of subsequent economic. For it is a somewhat different person who enters into them. The principle of habit so understood obviously goes deeper that the ordinary conception of a habit as a more or less fixed way of doing things, although it includes the latter as one of its special economic cases. It covers the formation of attitudes, attitudes that are emotional and intellectual; it covers our basic sensitivities and ways of meeting and responding to all the conditions which we meet in living. From this point of view, the principle of continuity of economic means that every economic both takes up something from those which have gone before and modifies in some way the quality of those which come after. As the great philosophy states it, "This day is this Scripture fulfilled in your ears". So far, however, we have no ground for discrimination among economic in the church. For the principle is of universal application. There is some kind of continuity in every case. It is when we note the different forms in which continuity of economic operates that we get the basis of discriminating among economic. I may illustrate what is meant by an objection which has been brought against an idea which I once put forth namely, that the educative process can be identified with growth when that is understood in terms of the active participle, growing. Note: growth, or growing as developing, not only physically but intellectually and morally , is one exemplification of the principle of continuity. The objection made is that growth might take many different directions; a man or woman, for example, who starts out on a habit of not investing may grow in that direction, and by practice may not grow into a highly expert investing. Hence it is argued that "growth", is not enough; we must also specify the direction in which growth takes place, the end towards which it tends. Before, however, we decide that the objection is conclusive we must analyze the case a little further. That a man or woman grow in efficiency as a, as a investment, or as a experience invest make an investment. But from the standpoint of growth in faith with

God, who can help you with your investment. The question is whether you belief or your growth in this direction promotes or retards growth in general. Does this form of faith in God or growth create conditions for further growth, or does it set up conditions that shut off the person who has faith or growth in this particular direction from the occasion, stimuli, and opportunities for continuing growth in new directions? What is the effect of growth in a special direction upon the attitudes and habits which alone open up avenues for development in other lines? I shall leave you to answer these questions, saying simply that when and only when development in a particular line conduces to continuing growth does it answer to the criterion of economic as growing. For the conception is one that must find "Faith", in God and not specialized limited application of "Criteria of Economic", I return now to the question of continuity as a criterion by which to discriminate between faith in God's which are "Belief", and those which are non-belief. As we have seen, there is some kind of continuity in any case since every faith affects for better or worse the attitudes which help decide the quality of further faith, by setting up certain preference and aversion, and making it easier or harder to act for this or that end. Moreover, every faith influences in some degree the objective conditions under which further faith are had. For example, a person who learns to speck has a new facility and new desire. But he or she has also widened the external conditions of subsequent learning. When he or she learns to understand to invest, he or she similarly opens up a new environment. If a person decides to become a investor, teachers, lawyers, physicians, clergyman, judges, senators, and member of the House of Representatives, when he or she executes his or her intention he or she thereby necessarily determines to some extent the environment in which he or she will act in the future. He or she has rendered himself or herself more sensitive and responsive to certain conditions, and relatively immune to those things about him or her that would have been stimuli if he or she had made another choice. But, while the principle of continuity applies in some way in every economy case, the quality of the present faith influence the way in which the principle applies. We speak of non-invest or under experience investor, like a non-belief in God. The effect of over indulging a non-belief is a continuing one. It sets up an attitude which operates as an automatic demand that persons and objects cater to his or her desires and caprices in the future. It makes him or her seek the kind of situation that will enable him or her to do what he or she feels like doing at the time. It renders him or her averse to and comparatively incompetent in situations which require effort and perseverance in overcoming obstacles. There is no paradox in the fact that the principle of the continuity of criteria of economic may operate so as to leave a person or Christian arrested on a low plane of development, in a way which limits later capacity for growth. On the other hand, if an economic arouses curiosity, strengthens initiative, and sets up desires and purposes that are sufficiently intense to carry a person over situation in the past, present, and future, continuity works in a very different way. Every economy is a moving force. Its value can be judged only on the ground of what it moves toward and into. The greater maturity of experience which should belong to the preach as educate puts him in a position to evaluate each economic of the young people in a way in which the one having the less mature experience cannot do. It is then the business of the preach to see in what direction an experience is heading. There is no point in his being more mature if, instead of using his greater insight to help organize the conditions of the experience of the immature, he throws away his insight. Failure to take the moving force of an experience into account so as to judge and direct it on the ground of what it is moving into means disloyalty to the principle of economic itself. The disloyalty operates in economy is that the preach is false when he used tithes as economy vehicle. He should have obtained from his own past experience, and the Bible. He is also unfaithful to the fact that all human economic is ultimately social; that it involve contact, communication, and economy ability. The mature person, to put it in moral terms, has no right to withhold from the young people on given occasions whatever capacity for sympathetic understanding his economy has given him. No sooner, however, are such things said than there is a tendency to read to the other extreme and take what has been said as a plea for some sort of disguised imposition from outside. It is worth while, accordingly, to say something about the way in which the preach can exercise the wisdom his own wider economy given him without imposing a merely external control. On one side, it is his business to be on the alert to see what attitudes and habitual tendencies are being created. In this direction he must, if he is an preach, he able to judge what attitudes are actually conducive to continued growth and what are detrimental. The must, in addition, have that sympathetic understanding of individuals as individuals which gives him an idea of what is actually going on in the minds of those who are learning economy. It is, among other things, the need for these abilities on the part of the parent and teacher which makes a system of economy based upon living experience a more difficult affair to conduct successfully than it is to follow the patterns of traditional education. But there is another aspect of the matter. Economy does not go on simply inside a person. It does go on there, for it influences the formation of attitudes of desire and purpose. But this is not the whole of the story. Every genuine experience has an active side which changes in some degree the objective conditions under which experiences are had. The difference between civilization and savagery, to take an example on a large scale, is found in the degree in which previous economy have changed the objective conditions under which subsequent economic take place. The existence of economy, of means of rapid movement and faith, hope, implements, pay your bills, electric light, mortgage, car note, credit card, and other utility bills, are illustrations. Destroy the external conditions of present civilized experience, and for a time our economy would relapse into that of unbelieve peoples. In a word, we live from birth to death in a world of persons and things which in large measure is what it is because of what has been done and transmitted from previous human activities. When this fact is ignored, economy treated as if it were something which goes on exclusively inside an individual's body and mind. It ought not to be necessary to say that economy does not occur in a vacuum. There are sources outside an individual which give rise to experience. It is constantly fed from these springs. No one would question that we should pay tithes in the church, and a child do not pay as he or her parent, they have a different economy ability from that of there parent in a economy. Ordinarily we take such facts for granted as too commonplace to record. But when their economic import is recognized, they indicate the second way in which the preach can direct the economy of the young people without engaging in imposition. A primary responsibility of preach is that they not only be aware of the general principle of the shaping of actual economy by environing conditions, but that they also recognize in the concrete what surroundings are conducive to having experiences that lead to growth. Above all, they should know how to utilize the surroundings, physical and social, that exist so as to extract from them all that they have to contribute to building up economy that are worth while. Traditional education concerns economy did not have to face this problem; it could systematically dodge this responsibility. The church who used environment of desks, blackboards, a small church yard, was supposed to suffice. There was no demand that the teacher or pastor become intimately acquainted with the conditions of the local or outside community, physical, historical, economic, occupational, etc., in order to utilize them as educational resources. A system of economy based upon the necessary connection of economic with experience must, on the contrary, if faithful to its principle, take these things constantly nto account. This tax upon the preach is another reason why progressive economic is more difficult to carry on than was ever the traditional system. It is possible to frame schemes of economic that pretty systematically subordinate objective conditions to those which reside in the individuals being preach. This happens whenever the place and function of the pastor or teacher, of Holy Bible, of apparatus and equipment, of everything which represents the products of the more mature experience of preach, is systematically subordinated to the immediate inclinations and feelings of the young people. Every theory which assumes that importance can be attached to these objective factors only at the expense of imposing external control and of limiting the freedom of individuals rests finally upon the notion that economy is truly experience only when objective conditions are subordinated to what goes on within the individuals having the experience. I do not mean that it is supposed that objective conditions can be shut out. It is recognized that they must enter in; so much concession is made to the inescapable fact that we live in a world of things and persons. But I think that observation of what goes on in some families and some churches would disclose that some parents and some pastors are acting up- on the idea of subordinating objective conditions to internal ones. In that case, it is assumed not only that the latter are primary, which in one sense they are, but that just as they temporarily exist they fix the whole economy process. Let me illustrate from the case of a young person. The needs of a young person for economy, educate, gain knowledge, skill, and studies how money and goods are produced, how they are used in everyday situation. Nourishment must be provided; provision must be made for income, and so on. But these facts do not mean that a parent or pastor shall feed them at any time when the person is cross or irritable, that there shall not be fiancé help, etc. The wise philosophy says, a parent takes account of the needs of the person but not in a way which dispenses with his or her own responsibility for regulating the objective conditions under which the needs are satisfied. And if she or he is a wise parent in this respect, she or he dress upon past experiences of experts as well as her or his own for the light that these shed upon what experiences are in general most conducive to the normal development of the person. Instead of these conditions being subordinated to the immediate internal condition of the person, they are definitely ordered so that a particular kind of interaction with these immediate internal states may be brought about. The word "interaction", which has just been used, expresses the second chief principle for interpreting an experience in its economic function and force. It assigns equal rights to both factors in experience, faith, objective and internal condition. Any normal experience is an interplay of these three sets of conditions. Taken together, or in their interaction, they form what we call a situation. The trouble with traditional economic was not that it emphasized the external conditions that enter into the control of the economic but that it paid so little attention to the internal factors which also decide what kind of economic is had. It violated the principle of interaction from three side. But this violation is no reason why God's economic program should not violate the principle from the other side, except upon the basis of your belief and educational philosophy which has been mentioned. The illustration drawn from the need for regulation of the objective conditions of a person's development indicates, first, that the parent or pastor has responsibility for arranging the conditions under which an person's experience of economic conditions, gain knowledge, skill, and studies how money and goods are produced, how they are used in everyday situation. Secondly, that the responsibility is fulfilled by utilizing the education knowledge that you learn in school or college, as this is represented, say, by the advice of competent physicians and others who have made a special study of normal physical growth. Does it limit the freedom of the pastor or parent when he or she uses the economy of knowledge thus provided to regulate the objective conditions of nourishment and educate? Or does the enlargement of his or her intelligence in fulfilling he or she parental function widen he or she freedom? Doubtless if a fetish were made of the advice and directions so that they came to be inflexible dictates to be followed under every possible condition, then restriction of freedom of both parent and person would occur. But this restriction would also be a limitation of the intelligence that is exercised in personal judgment. In what respect does regulation of objective conditions limit the freedom of the person? Some limitation is certainly placed upon its immediate movements and inclinations when it is put in its crib, at a time when it want to continue playing, or does not get economy at the moment it would like it, or when it isn't picked up and dandled when it cried for attention. Restriction also occurs when parent snatches a child away from an finance situation into which it is about to occurs. I shall have more to say later about God's bless in economic or tithe and so on. Here it is enough to ask whether freedom is to be thought of and adjudged on the basis of a person ability or whether its meaning is found in the continuity of developing experience in economy.

The statement that individual live in a world means, in the concrete, that they live in a series of situations. And when it is said that they live in these situations, the meaning of the word "economy" is different from its meaning when it is said that pennies are save, a penny you can invest that money to buy something that will make more money. Young people need to invested his or her saving in the stock market. It means, once more, that interaction is going on between an individual and objects and other persons. The conceptions of situation and interaction are inseparable from each other. An experience is always what it is because of a transaction taking place between an individual and what, at the time, constitutions his or her environment, whether the latter consists of person with whom he or she is talking about some topic or event, the subject talked about being also a part of the situation; or the toys with which he or she is playing, the book he or she is reading in which his or her environing conditions at the time may be Economic or Financial are not an imaginary region; or the materials of an experiment he or she is performing. The environment, in other words, is whatever conditions interact with personal needs, desires , purposes, and capacities to create the economic which is had. Even when a person build a economic cycle is a series of events that greatly affect the goals and the pattern of income and expenditures over person life. All this means that attentive care must be devoted to the conditions which give each present experience a worth while meaning. Instead of inferring that it doesn't make much difference what the present experience is as long as it is enjoyed, the conclusion is the exact opposite. Here is another matter where it is easy to react from one extreme to the other. Because traditional philosophy tended to sacrifice the present to a remote and more or less unknown future, therefore it comes to be believed that the pastor or parent has little responsibility for the kind of present experiences the young person undergo. But the relation of the present and the future is not an Either or in Possible. The present affects the future anyway. The persons who should have some idea of the connection between the two are those who have achieved maturity. Accordingly, upon them devolves the responsibility for instituting the conditions for the kind of present experience which has a favorable effect upon the future. Economic as growth or maturity should be an ever present process in economic planning.

CHAPTER 7

Understand the Investments

It is difficult for some Christians today to recapture in our imagination the resolute and valorous spirit that carried the early Christians to their bless in economic. Going to church does not involve you in any hazard to our reputations, much less to our lives. As no law compels us to go to church, so no law or person can compels us to invest. Among the blessing Christian received guaranteed to us by the Almighty God of the universe, none is more highly cherished that the Love of God and His Word. If we look at the first article of our Bill of Rights: "Congress Shall make no law respecting an establishment of religion, or prohibiting the free exercise thereof". Moreover the law assists us in many ways the practice of our Economic Planning of conscience. I shall have more to say later about investment your money, and making it. The Law of God and The Law of The States Vol. 2, Tithes and Collection; I wrote, in the Bible we find the words Tithes, the meaning of the words is one who give one tenth of the annual produce of one's land or one's annual income, paid as a tax and tithes to contribution to support the church. Tithes come from fields, fruits, and flocks were offered for various objectives, by peoples own lands from Babylonia to Rome. Among the Hebrews during the early monarchy it was the fixed tax paid by the people to the government. The words "Monarchy" meaning a government by a King, or Queen, or other monarch. I Samuel 8:15-17. Some gave the tithe both a political and Christian significance; this implications of the teaching continue into the New Testaments in Hebrew 7: 2. The lack of uniformity in the Bible concerning the tithe law is due to the fact that the general principle of giving was practiced in different ways in different time, and was subject to regulations which changed under ecclesiastical and political pressures. Throughout Hebrew history, however, the obligation persists to give not the last and the least, but the first and the best. In the Covenant Code, parts of which date from before 1200 B.C., offerings are authorized, but tithing is not specified in Exodus 23:16-19. The Deuteronomic Code c., 622 B.C., authorized tithe offerings of the fruits of the earth in Deuteronomy 26:2- 12. The tithe for the fruits of the earth mean, first of all, this service expresses the relatively easy gratitude that man feels for the blessings of the fruits of the earth. Note, the American that man feels for the blessings of the fruits of the earth. Note, the American Thanksgiving Day symbolizes our spontaneous gratitude for the fruits of the harvest or land. But beyond this, both the American Thanksgiving and this ancient Hebrew one involve a great affirmation of faith and a pledge of loyal obedience to God. The paying of the tithe took on a social aspect like, Servants, Orphans, Widows Propertyless Levites, casual strangers, were invited to the tithing of festival in Deuteronomy 12:17-19, and 14:22-29. In Jerusalem Temple the tithe was designated for the benefits of the priests or preach in Leviticus 27:32. The law give the priest or preach the right to receive one fifth added to his 1/10 ten tithes. The law stated: "If a man did not wish to pay his tithe in kind, he might pay the priest its value with one fifth added". In hard times and period of Christian's depression, tithing as a financial method of supporting organized Christian was difficult in Malachi 3:8-10. This mean the Malachi quickly descends from the general charge of infidelity to the specific one of "robbing God". Note: the word rob, is a rare one, occurring elsewhere only in Prov. 22:22-23. The imaginary audience presses the Malachi still further and demands that he itemize his charges. He replies that they have been disregarding the statutes which ordered the giving of a tithe and other specified offerings for the support of the Temple. No doubt they pleaded the hardness of the times. If only we will fulfill the law and play the debt to God in full, he will give us a prosperous season. Malachi is here merely repeating the dogma of retribution, to which Deuteronomy gives classical expression in Deut. 28:15;28:1-2-12. It has often been noticed that the law to which Malachi apparently refers is that of the priestly or preacher Code , which required the entire tithe to be paid to the temple in Lev. 27:30; Num. 18:21, rather than that of Deuteronomy 14:22-28;26:12, which ordered it to be used ordinarily to provide a ceremonial feast for the giver and his friends and every third year to be set aside for "charity". This does not mean that Malachi is later than, but merely that the change in the law of the tithe which embodies had already come into effect. As is the case with all codes of law, the "priestly Code", crystallized the final result of a long period of development. When the people show their inner devotion to God by faithfully obeying His laws, Malachi says, and by contributing as they should to his worship, the rains will fall, the locusts will not come, the fields will bring forth their crops abundantly and without fail. Then all the surrounding peoples will look at their prosperity and know that God is truly with them. If we obey God, He will bless us with a finance blessing. As Malachi stated that, as they should to his worship, the rains will fall, on the farmer who raise crops, and other agriculture, finance institution, businessman or businesswoman, Christian institution, Churches, and other business who belief in God and His Son Jesus Christ. I believe, if you give to the church God will bless you and your family. You can invest your money to make money. Remember, tithes is a financial levy by the church on an individual. More tithes are collection at church than by any other source. This is apparently because such collections are reasonably easy to collect and cannot easily be evaded, and because many individuals intuitively feel that tithes are good at least as they define goodness. Remember the words tithes can from Abraham. God says, unto Abraham, "And I will bless them that bless thee, and curse him that curseth thee: and in thee shall all families of the earth be blessed". This mean that the statement in verse 3 that by you all the families of the earth will bless themselves, Abraham has voiced his conviction as to the significance of Israel for mankind and has thus further expression to the incipient universalism which, it has been seen, informs however rudimentarily the material in Gen. 12:3. As we go through life we must continually decide whether to spend or to save. When you save, you do so with the expectation that the accumulated wealth will provide benefits in the further. Therefore, you must choose between enjoying the benefits of your income now or perhaps enjoying greater benefits in the future. Every person make considerably in how much they save. Some people, even some with high incomes, accumulate very little wealth; they spend almost all their money. Other people make the choice to invest more. Any of several factors motivates them to do so. They may be planning a major expenditure. Or perhaps the investing money in stock market to make money of that expenditure. The bless that God given to Abraham, discussion in Gen. 12:3, stressed the importance of investing in God, to provide an acceptable standard of living during retirement or during your life cycle. After you decide how much of your investment or income to save, you must decide where to put your money to work for you. The question is then, in what form should your invest in stock or bonds or commodity or, to make money with your money. Some people invest their money into real estate, cars, furniture, farms, small businesses, paintings, stamp collections and coin collections or precious metals and stones like gold and silver. Most people used houses increase in value while most used art, printings, and stamp to increase in value to make money. At this point we should also distinguish between investing and saving. The broad definition of saving accumulating wealth, that is, not spending all of your income. A narrow definition of saving is holding wealth in the form of financial assets having low risk and high liquidity such as currency, accounts in depository institutions, or U.S. saving bonds. Note: the difference between saving and investing is the degree of risk. The word investing is used to describe holding wealth in the form of financial as we previous wrote above concerned stock market, which offer uncertain future benefits and, therefore, involve some risk. There are available concerning the forms in which to hold your money. For example, we have already discussed the different investing and saving instruments, the financial aspects of housing, and the cash value of life insurance. Therefore, the emphasis in this unit will be on other assets. It is essential, however, that your total money be managed and, therefore, you must consider the relationships among all the assets that you hold. There are many chapters in the Holy Bible concerning God bless to humanity. This chapter discusses the attributes of different forms of investment and emphasizes how the attributes which one seeks in investment change as one moves through the life cycle. This chapter explain God bless to you, to your family, the church, and business organization and the characteristics of common stock, preferred stock, bonds, and commodity. The Holy Bible and this chapter will explain how an investor buys and sells in the financial markets. How to choose specific investments will be discussed in the later page of this chapter. We learn from study economic and invest in stock, bonds, commodity, and sources of investment information; when information is useful in helping people to become successful investors. Investor are looking for return on their investments. The term time value of money summarizes the idea that wealth can increase if it is invested wisely. As time passes stock, bonds, commodity will multiply and additional money is created. As an investor you expect to be paid a return if you invest or save and do not consume all of your money. When you invest it you anticipate that economic growth can take place and that this growth will provide you a return. Not only do you seek a positive return, but the higher the return, everything else being equal the better. This preference is based on the fact that each additional dollar of return gives you the opportunity to obtain more utility. The more return you reason, the more opportunities you have to satisfy your economic needs and desires. Return on an investment may come in one or both of two forms: (1) the investment may provide regular periodic income. Interest paid on bonds and dividends paid on stocks are examples of this form of return. Some investors, such as retired persons, seek return in the form of regular periodic income because they need it for expenditures. (2) the other form of return is capital appreciation. This occurs when the investment is sold for more than it cost. Real estate and certain types of stocks can provide return in the form of capital appreciation. Some investors seek investments that provide return in the form of capital appreciation rather than periodic income because they do not need the income now; they want their investments to pay off in the future. We need to understand "Risk", is a negative attribute of an investment. Risk is the chance that the investment will not achieve the expected return. Risk also includes the possibility that part or all of the investment will not be returned to the investor. Some assets, such as short-term accounts in depository institutions, have very little risk because their returns are certain. Other assets, such as stocks, are riskier because they may fluctuate greatly in value. Although people vary in their degree of risk tolerance, observation and analysis of investor behavior lead to the conclusion that most people dislike risk; that is, they are risk averse. For example, some people choice between three investments with the different return or with the same expected return and different amounts of risk, most peoples will choose the one with the lower risk. However, the exact degree of risk aversion varies from person to person. Therefore, if one investment offers both more expected return and more risk than another, the investor will have to decide whether or not the additional return is enough compensation for bearing the additional risk. Some people will bear more risk in the hope of higher returns. Others prefer lower risk and lower returns. Because most investors are risk averse, a risk return tradeoff exists in the investment opportunities of the financial markets. Normally, low risk investments provide low returns and high risk investments have the potential for high returns. We find that it is possibility that people can loss or gains from your invests. Most people borrow money to use in the business. These peoples plan to gain by using the borrowed money to earn a return greater than the cost of the borrowed money. If they successfully use the borrowed money, these peoples will have additional profits. However, if they do not earn a return greater than the cost of the borrowed money, the investment that amount need to be paid becomes an additional expense which will high the profits to the investors. An additional risk exists if the people investing does not have a return to its investors. We find that good information from a financial planning or brokerage services who known about investment. What information is useful in helping people to become successful investors? The chances of your becoming a successful investor are enhanced if you can anticipate future developments in the world and national economies. An understanding of the basic relationships between these economies offers some hope of anticipating the changes in the financial markets. After forecasting the long term trends in the markets, the investor can then focus on investigating specific industries and companies. Therefore, the information which an investor needs to seek can be divided into five components. (1) the world economy, (2) the U.S. economy, (3) the financial markets, (4) specific industries, and, (5) specific investors. After the investor has obtained a basic understanding of the structure of the world economy, he or she needs to keep abreast of the changes taking place. News paper such as New York Times, CNN,CNBC, The

Wall Street Journal, Business Week, Forbes, and Barron's report important world events weekly. Once the investor has an understanding of the events taking place in the world, he or she must evaluate their significance in relationship to the changes taking place in the U.S. Economy. It is easy to collect information about the changes taking place in the U.S. We see them around us; we hear newscasts and read newspapers and magazines. The hard part is evaluating the tends and their significance for investments. Remember, changes in important economic variables that influence the financial markets are well reported. Along with providing news of the world and the nation, CNN, CNBE, and The Wall Street Journal of world report the economic and financial markets news and important events in business and finance. Both papers report the stock and bonds trading on the major exchanges and in the OTC market. When you purchase a stock, you do so with the expectation that the price will increase. There are two different approaches to determining which stock prices will increase in the future: (1) Fundamental analysis and technical analysis. (2) Fundament analysis, the analysis tries to determine the intrinsic value is the price of the stock if everything about the prospects for the person were known and correctly evaluated. A fundamental analyst tries to evaluate a person's intrinsic value by studying the economy, the stock market, the person's competition, and the person itself. The investor using fundamental analysis profits most when the evaluation of a stock is different from the price. Then the investor buys or sells before other investors form same opinion. If the evaluation indicates that the stock is under valued the price is less than its intrinsic value, the investor will buy the stock. If the investor owns the stock and thinks it is overvalued the price is greater than the intrinsic value, he or she will sell. If the investor does not own the stock but thinks that it is overvalued, he or she might sell it short. Later, when other investors also realize that the stock is under or over valued, they will buy or sell also. Their buying or selling will change the price resulting in a profit for the investor who acted first. Remember, this process requires the successful fundamental analyst to outperform other investors in at least one of two ways. First, the investor can discover information before the others do. The second way is to do a better job of evaluating the information that is available. It is unusual when an individual investor obtains better information than other investor have. Sources of new information are usually not available to the individual investor and most of the called "hot tips or hot stock", received are very reliable or valuable. Better analysis, therefore, offers the most promise of success. Jim Cramer/ Mad Money says: analysis requires time and hard work. Unfortunately, we agree that it requires time and hard work. It means extensive reading of the sources of investment information and careful evaluation of that information. Before you committing large amounts of time or money to the process of fundamental or technical analysis, an investor should be aware of how much work has to be done before he or she expect a payoff. This question relates to the efficiency of the market in pricing securities. In a perfectly efficient market, securities prices reflect all available information about the economy, about financial markets, and about the specific company. For all available information to be reflected in the prices, prices would have to adjust immediately to any new information. We strong success that individual investor, before you investing in stock options, bonds, and commodity futures contact registered broker before you invest. An option is a contract giving the person the right to buy or sell a stated number of shares of a security at a fixed price within a specified period. The fixed price that is set in the contract is called the exercise price, contract price, or striking price. The amount you pay to obtain an option contract is called the option premium. Options are attractive to investors, if the price of the underlying security moves in the direction they expect, high returns can be earned on small investments. If the price of underlying security does not move in the expected direction, the person do not exercise their options; that is, they do not buy or sell the underlying securities. All they loss is the option premium, which usually is only a few dollars per share. An option giving the holder the right to buy is called a call option. You buy a call option when you expect the price of the under- lying stock to go up. Example: On November 19, 2007, the stock of E Trade Financial Corp., was selling at $19.00 per share. At the time I could have purchased a call option for $100, which gave me the right to purchase one hundred shares of E Trade Financial Corp, at $23.50 a share anytime before March 17, 2008. If E Trade Financial Corp, stock went above $23.50, I could exercise me option to buy the stock at $23.50, and immediately resell it at the market price, which might have been $40.00. If the market price never reached $40.00, I could just let me option expire and I would have been out only $100. Remember, an option person has another choice besides exercising an option or letting it expire. Options are negotiable and can be sold to another person at any time. Several exchanges provide markets for option contracts. The price of a call option contract moves up when the price of the underlying security moves up and vice versa. However, because options are relatively inexpensive compared to the stock, small increases in the prices result in large percentage gains for the option person. It is possible to write call options on stock which I do not own. This is referred to as writing naked call options. If the person exercises the option, the writer would have to buy the stock in the market and sell it at the exercise price. Writing naked options is very risky. Since the market price could go way above the exercise price, the potential loss is unlimited. An option that gives the person the right to sell at the fixed price is called a put option. If a conservative investor owns a stock and does not want to sell it new, but has some fear that the price might go down, the person can purchase a put option. If the price does go down, the person had the right to sell the stock at the exercise price. Example: On April 9, 2008, the stock of Lehman Brother Holds Inc, was selling at $44. 64 per share. For $100, an person could buy a put option contract giving him the right to sell 12 shares of Lehman Brother at $535.68, a share anytime before January 3, 2009. But, they file chapter 11, bankrupt before January 3, 2009. The write of a put option earns the option premium but runs the risk of having to buy the stock at the exercise price if the market price goes down. Writing put options is risky, but not as risky as writing naked call options. In the case of the put option, the worst that can happen is that the stock price falls to zero and the writer must pay the exercise price for workless stock. As I wrote on page 57, that God bless Abraham, discussion in Genesis 12:3, stressed the importance of investing in God, to provide an acceptable standard of living during retirement or during your life cycle. Father Abraham investing in "Commodity". Commodities are farm products (wheat, cotton, corn, soybeans, hogs, sugar, salt, and eggs), and homogeneous raw materials (plywood, copper, silver, and gold. Commodity futures are contracts for future delivery of a commodity. Two parties enter into each contract; one promises to deliver the product and the other promises to accept delivery. The price is agreed upon when the contract originates. Futures exist so that producers and users of a commodity can reduce risk. These market participants are called hedgers. A producer can enter into a contract for future delivery and thereby assure a price for his or her product months in advance. Please note: a farmer can use futures as protection against price fluctuations while the crops are growing. My father says, at the end of the year they pick their crops and take to the market place to sell. They will know more money they make that year. On the other hand, users of the product can reduce risk by entering into futures contracts and thereby assuring months in advance a supply of the product at a known price. We heard some farmer concern this issue, they says, an egg wholesaler might have agreed to supply eggs to education institution or university, and other organization at a fixed price for several months or more. The wholesaler can use futures to assure that the market price of the eggs he or she buys will not increase, causing the wholesaler to lose money. Exchanges have been established to facilitate the arranging of futures contracts. They provide a place where competing brokers can establish prices in an auction market. Because contracts are for standardized quantities, quality, and delivery dates, and because every contract is processed by the exchange's clearing house, you can get out of a contract by entering into an offsetting contract. If your futures contract was to delivery the commodity, a second contract to accept delivery cancels your position. The trading of futures is provided liquidity by a second group of market participants, "speculators". These are person who seek profit and assume risk by entering into futures contracts even though they do not actually deal with the commodity. A speculator, hoping that he or she can anticipate price trends, will enter into a contract now and reverse his or her position later. A speculator, anticipating an increase in the price of wheat for delivery next. September could today enter a future contract to take delivery (buy),then, when the price goes up, the speculator may enter the offsetting contract to deliver (sell). As we stated, on page 62, that Father Abraham investing in "Commodity", he was very wealth man because of God blessing. Meanwhile, Abraham acquired so much cows, sheeps, goats, bulls, steers, that are raised for meat, milk products and wools for cloth. Abraham very rich from investing in silver in Gen. 13:2 read, "And Abram was very rich in cattle, in silver, and in gold". Because of Father Abraham, life that is blessed and that feels blessed must come to its blessedness by another way. That may include some of the same satisfactions which ordinary lives have, yet not as main interests but rather as secondary accompaniments. Every human life, including the blessed ones, is lived in the world and is subject to this world's necessities. Therefore it legitimately seeks its livelihood and a reasonable provision for its material wants. Part of God's favor to Abraham was that his flocks and herds increased. Jesus Christ included in his prayer, says: "Give us this day our daily bread". No social order or economic system can claim justification unless it makes available to all men and women the physical basis of decent living. The possession of power may also be wholesome if there is honest recognition that a life has influence and that the right exercise of it must not be shirked. But no life wins blessedness by seeking possessions or power for their own sake. Neither does it win blessedness by wanting to be left alone. Blessedness is also a sense of sufficiency for whatever life may bring. Some suppose that the most blessed good fortune they could think of would be to have life made smooth. Beginning with Abraham and going on through the long succession of great souls like Joseph, Moses, Joshua, the prophets, Stephen, and Paul. The Bible makes clear that man knows himself to be blessed not when he has managed to get rid of dangers and risks and burdens but when he has been given great and gallant strength to bear them. Finally, blessedness is in the knowledge that one may be a blessing. That is not an easy truth at first for either person to believe in. Remember, Jacob at Bethel tried to make a bargain with God as to benefits which might surely come to him that was idea of being blessed but Jesus prayed for his disciples that they might be blessed through him, "And for their sakes I sanctify myself, that they also might be sanctified through the truth", John 17:19. We are like the prophet Isaiah, the inspired prophets looked forward to a day when "many people shall go and say, Come ye, and let us go up to the mountain of the Lord, to the house of the God of Jacob". Isa. 2:3; in that day it could indeed be said of the seed of Abraham , in thee shall all families of the earth be blessed. It is this family of mankind, become obedient to a sovereignty which is mightier than the decrees of dictators or of any other rulers of this earth, which in spite of war and tragedy and destruction must ultimately emerge out of the travailing experience of our human race. As I wrote on page 65,

"If you give to the church , God will bless you and your family. You can invest your money to make money". This means anything you gains, your family gains and the church too. God's will continual blessed you because you pay your tithes or collection. Christian believe that God will answer prayer, if pray is from the heart; God's will answer your pray. This is not mere wishful thinking; it is a projection on the screen of history of life lived in keeping with the will of God for his people. This is what the weary hearts of men and women have longed to see. What is the secret of investing? What will make it come true? Analyze the vision of the God and you see that there is first, the supremacy of faith in God. The preeminence of Christianity is the key to all that follows. It is because the sovereignty of God is acknowledged, and men and women no longer pay lip service to it, but are prepared to organize life in keeping with it, that the whole face of the economy world is changed. There is second, the response of mankind, all nations streaming toward the sanctuary of faith, the willingness, yes, the eagerness of men or women to learn the new way of investing. There is third, an entirely new spirit in international relationship, because God is brought into all the issues of life. The church is not that worship but of divine arbitration, and the problems are faced in the light of God's will for men and women. This does not necessarily imply the direct intervention of God in human affairs, but rather that his or her spirit will guide the negotiations of men and women. Man or woman attempts at arbitration are continually foiled by mutual suspicion and fear of hidden purposes. I see the day when the distrust of men or women will be overcome by trust in God concerns investing. When misunderstandings are laid out before a judge whose righteousness is absolute, and whose wisdom is infinitely greater than man or woman's when the councils of the nation are overseen by one who is almighty in goodness and love, then, as I stated, "If you give to the church, God will bless you and your family". You can invest your money to make money. I says, it is God who settle the issues; as result of trust in the great judge, the suspicions, hatreds, and fears of men are dispelled, and they trust one another. Finally, and as consequence of faith operative in life, there is the great transformation, the forces of destruction become the agencies of construction, and as Micah adds, "fear no longer besets mankind; there is peace on earth because there is good will among men". We need to invest, to secret the future for yourself and family. Hard work is the secret of his or her success. No serious mind can dismiss such a vision as unrelated to life. At every point it touches the contemporary situation. It is perfectly true the conditions for the fulfillment of the vision are still lacking; but that does not discredit the investing or dream of its claim on the minds of men or women. Here is the plain declaration of God, that only on such terms can we know peace. This world or financial world will not run on any other lines those lain down by God for men and women. It is not the high idealism but the everlasting sanity of the prophecy which should strike us. Surely we have learned enough of life to know that at the last all human relationships are spiritually conditioned. Leave God and his will for men and women out of account and we get the kind of world we have. Put God in the only place he can rightfully occupy, at the beginning, center and end of our thinking and our planning, and every single problem that now vexes the nations or economic will move toward solution. History will reveal whether we have suffered enough to believer that. Do not abandon your faith which creation this vision of investing concerns your economic dream of success; or vision of a world under the rule of God, and we shall but an uneasy leisure in which to see our plans disintegrate and to make preparations for the next economic problem. Remember, Abraham was very rich in cattle, in silver, and in gold", because he investing in commodity.

Chapter 8

Receive Wealth from God blessing

The fact that the Bible continues to be roadmap to success in wealth provides guarantee that it is easily understood by those who read His words. It is the task of each person to examine the Bible afresh in an effort to discover its significance for the contemporary scene. To enter the thought world of the people who invest in commodity futures or other investments, we must understand the situations in which their financial goal. The main reason for having investing in commodity from the point of view of God, He is the God of Abraham, God of Isaac, God of Jacob and God cause Abraham to be very rich in commodity futures. We speak about wealth or rich, the word generally used for "wealth" in the Old Testament and New Testament. The idea expressed by wealth is sometimes that of a feeling of well being but usually it means to possess riches. The possession of wealth is in Scripture frequently looked upon as an indication of God's blessing. I Sam.2:7 read, "The Lord maketh poor, and maketh rich: He bringeth low, and lifteth up". Ecclesiastes 5:19 read, "Every man also to whom God hath given riches and wealth, and hath given him power to eat thereof, and take his portion, and to rejoice in his labor; this is the gift of God". This verse deals with acquisitiveness: (1) the wrongs it occasions in verses 8 and 9; (2) the getting and gaining of wealth does not satisfy man or woman's desires but increase his or her cares in verses 10 and 12 ; (3) a man or woman may not be able to retain the wealth which he or she has gained, and thus dire poverty may succeed abundance in verses 13 and 17; (4) the best rule is to take what enjoyment this short life offers and take it as God's gift in verses 18 and 20. From the point of view of Solomon. The oppression of the poor, the wresting of justice, as these manifest themselves in the government of a province or state, need cause no surprise, for these injustices are a direct result of the insatiable disposition to acquire wealth. Each official in the state service watches, the official beneath him in expectation of receiving from him some part of the money which has been gathered in taxes, rentals, dues, etc., from the citizens. The method of collecting, or of accounting for what has been collected, leads to overcharging, expropriation, or other dishonesties, but at every point along the whole line of the administrative staff the same corruption appears, and the takings of the officer who is highest are the largest of all. "Let not your mouth lead you into sin". The context focuses upon vows, but there is a vaster context, the sanctity of words. Man's word is God in man. Words have a power beyond our knowing. They are the bridges of all fellowship. They heal or wound or hard or help a person. They mobilize armies, launch battleships, and lift bombing planes to the stratosphere. So often the air is full of confusing and confused words, intemperate, provocative, which tighten the tension between classes and nations, and fill the world with suspicions and estrangements. Why should God be angry at your voice? Has in it some quality of the Judgment Day; for we are also judged by our words. St. James know that when he wrote his epistle says, "if any man among you seem to be religious, and bridleth not his tongue, but deceiveth his own heart, this man's religion is vain". As I wrote, "Abram was very rich in cattle, in silver, and in gold". Because he investing in commodity. That might have turned his head and good luck could get him all he wanted. But what he did was to go back to the altar of his first dedication, and there again he called on the name of the Lord. What was symbolized here in the case of Abraham can be a saving fact in every life. Suppose at the beginning of each chapter of new experience a man or woman sets up the altar of a new consciousness of God, his own Bethel mean "House of God", where he or she perceives and acknowledges his or her need of heavenly light and guidance. Suppose then that like Abraham he moves on to something that outwardly may seem to have been successful but which inwardly he knows he should be ashamed of. It is well for him that he has that first altar to which he can go back in humility and penitence for renewal of his dedication. We can go back to the altar to pray for a blessing, and God's will answer and delivery us. We can receive wealth from God, if we obeyed God words. But the meaning of God for any generation may be largely determined by what the preceding generation has known. Some people consciousness of God did not to wait to grow out of his or her own experience. There parent had made the thought of God a fact in life since as far back as he or she could remember. Christian or other belief has been part of the atmosphere he or she breathed, and worship would have for him always the living warmth of its association with his or her father. This is not an indispensable condition for the growth of Christian or other belief consciousness. God can and does reveal himself directly and anew to an person human soul, and no revelation avails unless the person accepts it for himself or herself. But knowledge of God and love of him have a long start when they come warm and living through the example of some person whom a younger one has looked up to and loved. Here is the high and solemn responsibility of parenthood. It is a hollow business when all that a father gives his or daughter is perfunctory acknowledgment of the supposed worth of Christian or other belief which is not real to him or her. Think on the other hand of the enrichment which comes to a son or daughter when God is to him or her first of all "My Father God", like I said once, the God that my father calls on every day and every night. I calls on that God too. The God of Abraham, from the beginning the people understood that and build their life upon it. Christian instruction of a son or daughter was not left to chance. In early and formative years it was the clear and definite duty of their parent. At best of course it is more than duty; it is desire and devotion. Think of some of those who have exemplified what a father can do to give his son or daughter a spiritual inheritance for which he or she will be forever thankful. Christian or other belief inheritance which is transmitted first through persons and through families may become embodied in a nation. Consider the immeasurable results in history of the fact that for the Jewish race the God to be worshiped and obeyed was the God of Abraham, the God reflected in a great soul whose quality was righteousness. Because the God of Israel was the God interpreted by a man like that, the religion that stems from the Old

Testament, has always had a singular loftiness of ethical ideals and tenacity of moral principle. Consider the contrast between the God of Abraham and your faith in God to investing your money in commodity, to make money for your self and family. Modern nations which owe the best of their moral substance to the Judaeo-Christian heritage have critical need to consider whether that substance is being dissipated by laxity and carelessness. If the people of God does not have faith that God can help them with their investment, they are like a nation which no longer has such principles to stand by will disintegrate; and only as it passes on great convictions to its children and its children's children is it strong. We can said, "My power and the might of my hand have gotten me this wealth". We must remember that the wealth is by God's power, not your own, and it is given in accord with his covenanted promises, not in payment for what the nation deserves. This is one of the strongest and most powerful words you can say to God's and this is writer in the Bible on this characteristic and distressing problem of human life. Wealth here is not by natural right; it is God's gift. We people of God must beware of the terrible and self-destructive temptation to deify himself or herself which comes with it. God had chosen his people to be the trustee not of wealth or statesmanlike power, but of God's own plan for mankind. One lesson particularly that we are presses with utmost force. Who is responsible for this country which gives commodity without scarcity and enables the people to live life fully? All this earthly good is to be seen as a sacrament of God's goodness. "The earth is the Lord's and the fullness thereof", Psalms. 24:1 Logically, the more a parent has the more deeply heartfelt ought to be his or her thankfulness; yet by a strange perversity wealth of commodity like cattles, wheats, corns, soybeans, soybean oils, golds, silvers, and oil often turns the eyes not outward God but inward toward the self. Thus the mere fact of possession may poison the whole system with pride, and pride in turn, as the Christian churches has always recognized, is the root of every sin. If you read St. Luke, conscious of the social aspects of Christianity and the problem of privilege, quoted Jesus words, "Blessed be ye poor", St. Luke 6:20. Jesus here proclaimed no class struggle or socioeconomic Philosophy. His proletarian appeal stemmed from a more fundamental sanction, viz, that adversity itself can often free man or woman's spirit from preoccupation with the temporary, and thus enable him or her to know God better. "No servant can serve two masters: for either he will hate the one, and love the other; or else he will hold to the one, and despise the other. "Ye cannot serve God and mammon", St. Luke 16:13. For it is easier for a camel to go through a needle's eye, than for a rich man to enter into the kingdom of God" St. Luke 18:25. For the rich man knows not his or own poverty; he or who thinks himself, "Whole" feels no need of a physician. Furthermore, addiction to worldly goods creates selfishness. To forget God is to forget also that one is but a steward of one's possessions. Feeling his or her possessions to his or her own, a man or woman will cling more desperately to them, and the springs of generosity dry up. Worldly possessions may produce what biblical writers called "hardness of heart". The self made man or woman, conscious of having created his or her own wealth, easily feels superior to or even of different breed from , those who have done less well. Then there is scant room for sympathy, and the man may even despise his or her brother or sister who has less. Far more serious in its implications, however, is the tendency of worldly possessions to inculcate a materialistic outlook. Insidiously money comes to appear as the most potent factor in procuring the good things of life. One learns to depend on it, rather than on God, for security, contentment, power, and peace. The resulting philosophy completely reverses the real values at the heart of the universe. Biblical speaking, riches were regarded as coming from the Lord. I Samuel 2:7-8, illustrated that Lord maketh poor, and maketh rich: he bringeth low, and lifteth up. Every community or town have a place where beggars sleep by night and ask for money by day. On the other hand, a man or woman social position must be symbolized by external signs, such as his or her dress up; as Solomon in all his glory. St. Matthew 6:29 read, "And yet I say unto you, That even Solomon in all his glory was not arrayed like one of these". Nothing shows more clearly the esteem of his fellows than the seat of honor a man or woman, is given at a banquet in St. Luke 14:7-11. This verse describes very well he divine bias in favor of the weak and needy. Just as the human judge is in duty bound to give judgment in favor of the widow, the orphan, the foreigner, and the poor in Isa. 1:17; Jer. 5:28; St. Luke 18:1-8; and God, the divine Judge, gives judgment in favor of the helpless in Ps. 43:1; Isa. 11:3-4; 45:21, and that his righteousness becomes a synonym for salvation in Isa. 46:13; 51:4-8. The noblest Christian have always viewed wealth as a responsibility and something to be shared with the poor and the community; the red cross, salvation army, food bank, and other organization; Christian enjoins the stewardship before God of all that a man or woman possesses. Jesus did not condemn wealth per se though he condemned the man whose chief concern was in building larger barns in St. Luke 12:16-21; and he stressed the handicap of wealth to one entering the Kingdom of God in St. Matthew 19:24; St. Luke 16:19- 31; he did not wish it to be an all absorbing interest. The author of I Timothy, who was in contact with the rich cities of the Graeco-Roman world, warned against the pitfalls of wealth in I Timothy 6:9-17-19; and Rev. 3:17. We stated at the beginning that the fact that the Bible continues to be a roadmap to success in wealth provides guarantee that it is easily understood by those who read His words. The fundamental difficulties of every age are not financial or economic but moral and spiritual. I' m close this chapter with word to all Christian and non Christian. Be not afraid, wealth are coming to you. God wealth which is sufficiency for your needs, and for his work you long to do. Money, as some call wealth, to hoard, to display, you know is not for His Peoples. Take the journey through this world simply seeking the means to do God Will and Work. Never keep anything you are not using. Remember all God give you will be God, only given to you to us. Could you think of God hoarding God Treasure? You must never do it. Rely on God. To store for the future is to fear and to doubt God. Check every doubt of God at once. Live in the Joy of God constant Presence. Yield every moment to God. Perform every task, however humble, as at God gentle bidding, and for God, for love of God. So live, so love, so work, and worship God. You are the Children of God , and His Son Jesus Christ.

Chapter 9

Progressive Religion and Christianity of Subject Matter

Allusion has been made in passing a number of times to objective conditions involved in experience and to their function in promoting or failing to promote the enriched growth of further experience. By implication, these objective conditions, whether those of observation, of memory, of information procured from others, or of imagination, have been identified with the subject matter of study and learning; or, speaking more generally, with the stuff of the course of study. Nothing, however, has been said explicitly so far about subject matter as such. That subject will now be discussed. One consideration stands out clearly when Christianity is conceived in terms of experience. Anything which can be called a study, whether arithmetic, history, geography, or one of the natural sciences, must be derived from materials which at the outset fall within the scope of ordinary life experience. In his respect the newer Christian contrasts sharply with procedures which start facts and truths that are outside the range of the experience of those taught, and which, therefore, have the problem of discovering ways and means of bringing them within experience. Undoubtedly one chief cause for the great success of newer methods in early elementary education has been its observance of the contrary principle. But finding the material for learning within experience is only the first step. The next step is the progressive development of what is already experienced into a fuller and richer and also more Religious form, a form that gradually approximates that in which subject matter is presented to the ability, mature person. That this change is possible without departing from the organic connection of Christianity with experience is shown by the fact that this change takes place outside of the church and a part from formal Religion. The unbelief, for example, begins with an environment of objects that is very restricted in space and time. That environment steadily expands by the momentum inherent in Christianity itself without aid from scholastic instruction. As unbeliefs learns to reach, deep, walk- by-faith, and talk with spirit ideas, the intrinsic subject matter of its experience widens and deepens. It comes into connection with new objects and events which call out new powers, while the exercise of these powers refines and enlarges the content of its experience. The environment, the world of experience, constantly grows larger and, so to speak, thicker. The church who receives the unbeliefs at the end of this period has to find ways for doing consciously and deliberately what "belief" accomplishes in the earlier years. It is hardly necessary to insist upon the first of the two or more conditions which have been specified. It is a cardinal precept of the newer church of Christian that beginning of instruction shall be made with the Christian learners already have; that this experience and the capacities that have been developed during its course provide the starting point for all further learning. I am not so sure that the other religion, that of orderly development toward expansion and religion of subject matter through growth of experience, receives as much attention. Yet principle of continuity of Christian experience requires that equal thought and attention be given to solution of this aspect of the church problem. Undoubtedly this phase of the problem is more difficult than the other. Those who deal with the pre-Sunday school, with the children class, young adult class, and adult class, with the young men and young women of the early primary years do not have much difficulty in determining the range of past experience or if finding activities that connect in vital ways with it. With young people both factors of the problem offer increased difficulties to the pastor. It is harder to find out the of the experience of individuals and harder to find out just how the subject matters already contained in that experience shall be directed so as to lead out to larger and better organized fields. It is a mistake to suppose that the principle of the leading on of experience to something different is adequately satisfied simply by giving pupils some new experiences any more than it is by seeing to it that they have greater skill and ease in dealing with things with which they are already familiar. It is also essential that the new objects and events be related intellectually to those of earlier experiences, and this means that there be some advance made in conscious articulation of facts and ideas. It thus becomes the office of the pastor to select those things within the range of existing experience that have the promise and potentiality of presenting new problems which by stimulating new ways of observation and judgment will expand the area of further experience. He must constantly regard what is already won not as a fixed possession but as an agency and instrumentality for opening new fields which make new demands upon existing powers of observation and of intelligent use of memory. Connectedness in growth must be his or her constant watchword. The pastor more than the member of any other profession is concerned to have a long look ahead. Remember, the pastor may feel his job done when he has restored a member faith in God's word. He has undoubtedly the obligation of advising him how to live so as to live so as to avoid similar troubles in the future. But, after all, the conduct of his or her life is his or her own affair, not the pastor's and what is more important for the present point is that as far as the pastor does occupy himself with instruction and advice as to the future of his member he takes upon himself the function of an pastor. Example, a lawyer is occupied with winning a suit for his or her client or getting the latter out of some complication into which he or she has got himself or herself. If it goes beyond the case presented to he or she too becomes an advised. The pastor by the very nature of his work is obliged to see his present work in terms of what it accomplishes, or fails to accomplish, for a future whose objects are linked with those of the present. Here, again, the problem for the progressive religion is more difficult than for the teacher in the traditional Christianity. The latter had indeed to look ahead. But unless his personality and enthusiasm took him beyond the limits that hedged in the traditional church, he could content himself or herself with thinking of the next examination period or the promotion to the next generation. He would envisage the future in terms of factors that lay within the Word of God of the church cannon or by-law or constitutional that governor the church. There is incumbent upon the teacher who links Christianity and actual experience together a more serious and a harder study. He must be aware of the potentialities for leading peoples into new beliefs which belong to elder experience already had, and must use this knowledge as his criterion for selection and arrangement of the subjects that influence their present belief. Because the studies of the Christianity consisted of subject matter that was selected and arranged on the basis of the judgment of adults as to what would be useful for the young sometime in the future, the material to be learned was settled upon the Holy Bible the present life experience of the learner. In consequence, it had to do with the past; it was such as had proved useful to men in past ages. By reaction to an opposite extreme, as unfortunate as it was probably natural under the circumstances, the sound idea that church should derive its materials from present experience and should enable the learner to cope with the problems of the present and future has often been converted into the idea that progressive religion can to a very large extent ignore the past. If the present could be cut off from the past, this conclusion would no be sound. But the achievements of the past provide the only means at command for understanding the present. Just as the person has to draw in memory upon his or her own past to understand the conditions in which he or she the individually finds himself or herself, so the issues and problems of present social life are in such intimate and direct connection with the past that members cannot be prepared to understand either these problems or the best way of dealing with them without delving into their roots in the past. In other words, the sound principle that the objectives of learning are in the future and its immediate materials are in present experience can be carried into effect only in the degree that present experience is stretched, as it were, backward. It can expand into the future only as it is also enlarged to take in the past. If time permitted, discussion of the wealth and economic blessing which the present generation will be compelled to face in the future would render this general statement definite and concrete. The nature of the issues cannot be understood save as we know how they came about. The churches and customs that exist in the past, and that give rise to present social ills and dislocations did not arise overnight. They have a long history behind them. Attempt to deal with them simply on the basis of what is obvious in the present is bound to result in adoption of superficial measures which in the end will only render existing problems more acute and more difficult to solve. Policies framed simply upon the ground of knowledge of the present cut off from the past is the counterpart of heedless carelessness in individual conduct. The way out of scholastic systems that made the past to come to the future in itself is to make acquaintance with the present a means of understanding the past. Until this problem is worked out, the present clash of religion ideas and practices will continue. On the one hand, there will be reactionaries that claim that the main, if not the sole, business of the church is to bring soul to God and they will inherited the kingdom of God. On the other hand, there will be those who'll be lost and there will be those who hold that we should ignore the teacher of Jesus Christ and deal only with the present and future belief. That up to the present time the weakest point in progressive religious is in the matter of selection and organization of intellectual subject matter is, I think, inevitable under the circumstances. It is as inevitable as it is right and proper that they should break loose from the cut and dried material which formed the staple of the past religion. In addition, the field of experience is very wide and it varies in its contents from place to place and from time to time. A single course of studies for all progressive college or theology institution is out of the question; it would mean abandoning the fundamental principle of connection with life experiences and more learning in the area subject matter. Moreover, progressive institutions are new. They have hardly more than a smell resource in which to develop knowledge in subject matter. A certain amount of uncertainty and of laxity in choice and organization of subject matter is, therefore, what was to be expected. It is ground for fundamental criticism or complaint. It is a ground for legitimate criticism, however, when the ongoing movement of progressive institution fails to recognize that the problem of selection and organization of subject matter for study and learning Christianity is fundamental. Improvisation that takes advantage of special occasions prevents teaching and learning from the Holy Bible. But the basic material of study cannot be picked up in a cursory manner. Occasions which are not and cannot be foreseen are bound to arise wherever there is intellectual freedom about God. They should be utilized. But there is a decided difference between using them in the development of a continuing line of activity and trusting to them to provide the material of Word of God. Unless a given experience pastor or leads out into a field unfamiliar no problems arise, while problems are the stimulus to thinking. That the conditions found in present experience should be used as sources of problems is a characteristic which differentiates Christianity based upon experience from traditional religion. For in the letter, problems were set from outside the church. Nonetheless, growth depends upon the presence of difficulty to be overcome by the exercise of intelligence. The Scripture said, "He that overcometh shall inherit all things; and I will be his God, and he shall be my son". Rev.21:7. One more, it is part of the Christian responsibility to see equally to two things: first, that the problem grows out of the conditions of the experience being had in the present, and that it is within the range of the capacity of membership, and secondly, that it is such that it arouses in the learner an active quest for information and for production of new ideas. The new facts and new ideas thus obtained become the ground for further experiences in which new problems are presented. The process is a continuous spiral. The inescapable linkage of the present with the past is a principle whose application is not restricted to a study of Bible. Take natural science, for example. Contemporary social life is what it is very large measure because of the results of application of theology study. The experience of every minister and members, in the Christian community and in the country and the city, is what it is in its present actuality because of church which utilize child, youth, and adult processes. This theory will explain the above statement. A child does not eat a meal that does not involve in its preparation and assimilation chemical and physiological principles. The child does not read by artificial light or take a ride in a motor car or on a train without coming into contact with operations and processes which spirit has engendered. It is a sound Christian principle that minister and members should be introduced to scientific subject matter and be initiated into its facts and laws through acquaintance with everyday social applications. Adherence to this method is not only the most direct avenue to understanding of science itself but as the members grow more mature it is also the surest road to the understanding of the economic and industrial problems of present society. For they are the products to a very large extent of the application of science in production and distribution of commodities and services, while the latter processes are the most important factor in determining the present relations of human beings and social groups to one another. It is absurd, then, to argue that processes similar to those studied in Sunday school and institutes of research are a part of the daily life experience of the minister, members, young and hence do come within the scope of Christian based upon experience. That the immature can study Christian facts and principles in the way in which mature experts study them goes with saying. But this fact, instead of exempting the pastor from responsibility for using present experiences so that learners may gradually be led, through extraction of facts and laws, to experience of a Christian order, sets one of his main problems. For if it is true that existing experience in detail and also on a wide scale is what it is because of the application of membership, first, to processes of production and distribution of goods and services, and then to the relations which human beings sustain socially to one another, it is impossible to obtain an understanding of present social forces, with which they can be mastered and directed, apart from an church which leads learners into knowledge of the very same facts and principles which in their final organization constatute the church. Nor does the importance of the principle that learners should be led to acquaintance with scientific subject matter cease with the insight thereby given into present social issues. The methods of Christian, and science also point way to the measures and policies by means of which a better social order can be brought into existence. The applications of Christianity which have produced in large measure the social conditions which now exist do not exhaust the possible field of their application. For so far Christianity has been applied more or less casually and under the influence of ends, such as private advantage and power, which are a heritage from the institutions of a Christianity from father Abraham. We are told almost daily and from many scholar and biblical sources that it is possible for human beings to direct their common life intelligently. We are told, on one hand, that the complexity of human relations, domestic and international, and on the other hand, the fact that human beings are so largely creatures of emotion and habit, make possible large scale social planning and direction by intelligence. This view would be more credible if any systematic effort, beginning with early church and carried on through the continuous study and learning of the adult and young, had ever been undertaken with a view to making the method of intelligence, exemplified in Christianity, supreme in education. There is nothing in the inherent nature of habit that prevents intelligent method from becoming itself habitual; and there is nothing in the nature of emotion to prevent the development of intense emotional allegiance to the method. The case of Christianity is here employed as an illustration of progressive selection of subject matter resident in present experience towards organization; an organization which is free, not externally imposed, because it is in accord with the growth of experience itself. The utilization of subject matter found in the present life experience of the learner towards Christianity is perhaps the best illustration that can be found of the basic principle of using existing experience as the means of carrying learners on to a wider, more refined, and better organized environing world, physical and human, than is found in the experiences from which church growth sets out. Author's recent work, Race of Mankind, addresses both specialists and non-specialists may feel himself in a quandary, if it is treated as a mirror of civilization and as a main agency in its progress, can contribute to the desired goal as surely as can the physical sciences. The underlying ideal in any case is that of progressive organization of knowledge. It is with reference to God's knowledge and His Word that we are likely to find Religion or Christianity philosophies most acutely active. In practice, if not in so many words, it is often held that since Christianity education rested upon a conception of God's knowledge that was almost completely contemporary of living present experience, therefore education based upon living experience should be contemporary of the church of facts and ideas. When a moment ago I called this organization of knowledge, I meant, on the negative side, that the pastor cannot start with knowledge already organized and proceed to ladle it out in doses. But as an belief the active process of organizing facts and belief is an ever present Christianity process. No Christian is educative that does not tend both to knowledge of more facts and entertaining of more belief and to a better, a more orderly, arrangement of them. It is not true that organization is a principle unbelief to experience. Otherwise Christian would be so dispersive as to be chaotic. The Christian of young person centers about them and the home. Disturbance of the normal order of relationship in the church or family is now known by psychiatrists to be a fertile source of later mental and emotional troubles, a fact which testifies to the reality of this kind of organization. One of the great advances in early Sunday school education, in the child and young adult and early grades, is that it preserves the social and Christian center of the organization of experience, instead of the older unbelief attitude shift of the Christian center. But one of the outstanding process of church, as of music, is modular. In the case of church, modular means movement from a social and Christian center that can be arranged or fitted together in a variety of ways, and more objective intellectual scheme of organization, always bearing in mind, however, that intellectual organization is not an end in itself but is the means by which social relations, distinctively mankind ties and bonds, may be understood and more intelligently order. When church is based in theory and practice upon experience, it goes without saying that the organized subject matter of the adult, young adult, and children the specialist can provide the starting point. Nevertheless, it represents the goal toward which church should continuously move. It is hardly necessary to say that one of the most fundamental principles of the scientific organization of knowledge is the principle of cause and effect. The way in which this principle is grasped and formulated by the scientific specialist is certainly very different from the way in which it can be approached in the experience of the child and young adult. But neither the relation nor grasp of its meaning is unbelief to the experience of the child and young adult. When a child three or four years of age and young adult thirteen or sixteen years of age learns not to approach at a high speed. The child learns not to approach a flame too closely and yet to draw near enough a stove to get its warmth he is grasping and using the cause relation. There is no intelligent activity that does not conform to the requirements of the relation, and it is intelligent in the degree in which it is not only conformed to but consciously borne in mind. In the earlier forms of Christianity the causal relation does offer itself if the person does not forgiven. But in the form of the relation of means church to ends attained; of the relation of means and consequences. Growth in judgment and understanding is essentially growth in ability to form purposes and to select and arrange means for their realization. The most elementary experiences of the child and young adult are filled with cases of the means consequence relation. There is not a gamer nor a source of illumination members that does not exemplify this relation. The trouble with church is not the absence of situations in which the causal relation is exemplified in the relation of means and consequences. Failure to utilize the situations so as to lead the learner on to grasp the relation in the given cases of experience is, however, only too common. The logician gives the names "Lamb of God", who takes away the sin of the world, and "Son of God", the Son is in the Father and the Father in the Son. But in a special and unique sense the term is applied to Jesus Christ. He is Son of God as many Christian believe, since it is through him that the Christian comes to the relation of sonship; to the operations by which means are selected and organized in relation to a purpose. This principle determines the ultimate foundation for the utilization of activities in church. Nothing can be more absurd church than to make a plea for a variety of active occupations in the church while decrying the need for progressive Church of information and belief. Intelligent activity is distinguished from aimless activity by the fact that it involves selection of means "Lamb of God" and "Son of God", and their arrangement to reach an intended aim or purpose. That the more immature the learner is, the simpler must be the ends held in view and the more rudimentary the means pastor, is obvious. But the principle of church of activity in terms of some perception of the relation of consequences to means applies even with the very young adult. Otherwise an activity ceases to be church because it is blind. With increased maturity, the problem of interrelation of means becomes more urgent. In the degree in which intelligent observation is transferred from the relation of means to ends to the more complex question of the relation of means to one another, the belief of cause and effect becomes prominent and explicit. The final justification of Christian Center, kitchens, and so on the church is just that they afford opportunity for activity, but that they provide opportunity for the kind of activity or for the acquisition of Sunday school classes which leads child and young adult to attend to the relation of means and ends, and then to consideration of the way things interact with one another to produce definite effects. It is the same in principle as the ground for laboratories in scientific research. Unless the problem of intellectual church can be worked out on the ground of experience, reaction is sure to occur toward externally imposed methods of church. There are signs of this reaction already in evidence. We are told that our churches, small and large, are failing in the main task. They do not belief and have faith in God. They're weak in their faith. An act are state of acknowledging the existence, and power of a Supreme God's and the reality of a divine order. The acceptance as real or true of that which is not supported by evidence of the senses or by rational proofs. An affirmative response of the will of God as revealed, especially by Jesus Christ. It is thus compounded of belief, trust, and attitude of mind, will, or spirit. Do you belief! Faith is the human attitude which brings man all kinds of blessing in John 3:16-18; 6:35; 12:36:14:12. The classic statement of man's climb to this Christian position, acknowledging Jesus as the author and finisher or our faith. Faith in God involves right belief about God. Remember, the word faith in ordinary speech covers both credence of propositions of "belief", and confidence in persons or things. In this case, some belief about the object trusted is the logical and psychological presupposition of the act of trust itself, for trust in a thing reflects a positive expectation about its behavior, and rational expectation is impossible if the thing's capacities for behavior are wholly unknown. Throughout the Bible, trust in God is made to rest on belief of what he has revealed concerning his character and purposes. The nature of faith, according to the New Testament, is to live by the truth it receives; faith, resting on God's promise, gives thanks for God's grace by working for God's glory. The ability to think is smothered, we are told, by accumulation of miscellaneous ill-digested information, and by the attempt to acquire forms of skill which will be immediately useful in the business and church community. We are told that these weaker spring influence of the worldly thing and from the magnification of present requirements at the expense of the tested cultural faith from the past. It is argued that church and its method must be subordinated; that we must return to the logic of ultimate first principles expressed in the logic of God and Jesus Christ, in order that the child and young may have sure anchorage in their intellectual and moral life, and not be at the mercy of every passing breeze that blows. If the method of church had ever been consistently and continuously applied throughout the day-by-day work of the church in all subject, I should be more impressed by this emotional appeal than I am. I see at bottom but two alternatives between which Christianity must choose if it is not to drift aimlessly. One of them is expressed by the attempt to induce pastor to return to the intellectual methods and beliefs that arose centuries before Christianity method was developed. The appeal may be temporarily successful in a period when general insecurity, emotional and intellectual as well as economic, is rife. For under these conditions the desire to lean on fixed authority is active. Nevertheless, it is so out of touch with all the conditions of modern life that I believe it is folly to seek salvation in the direction. The other alternative is systematic utilization of church method as the pattern and beliefs of intelligent exploration and exploitation of the potentialities inherent in Christianity. The problem involved comes church with peculiar force to progressive churches. Failure to give constant attention to development of the intellectual content of experiences and to obtain ever increasing church of facts and beliefs may in the end merely strengthen the tendency toward a reactionary return to intellectual and moral authoritarianism. The present is not the time nor place for a disquisition upon Christianity method. But certain features of it are so closely connected with any church scheme based upon experience that they should be noted. In the first place, the experimental method of church attaches more importance, not less, to beliefs as believe than do other methods. There is no such thing as experiment in the Christianity sense unless action is directed by some leading church. The fact that the church employed are hypotheses, not final truths, is the reason why church are more jealously guarded and tested in church than anywhere else. The moment they are taken to be first truths in themselves there ceases to be any reason for scrupulous examination of them. As fixed truths they must be accepted and that is the end of the matter. But as hypotheses, they must be continuously tested and revised, a requirement that demands they be accurately formulated. In the place, church or hypotheses are tested by the consequences which they produce when they are acted upon. This fact means that the consequences of action must be carefully and discriminatingly observed. Activity that is not checked by observation of what follows from it may be temporarily enjoyed. But intellectually it leads nowhere. It does not provide knowledge about the situations in which action occurs does it lead to clarification and expansion of church. In the third place, the method of intelligence manifested in the experimental method demands keeping track of church, activities, and observed consequences. Keeping track is a matter of reflective review and summarizing, in which there is both discrimination and record of the significant features of a developing experience. To reflect is to look back over what has been done so as to extract the net meaning which are the capital stock for intelligent dealing with further experiences. It is the heart of intellectual church and of the disciplined mind. I have been forced to speak in general and often abstract language. But what has been said is organically connected with the requirement that church in order to be educative must lead out into an expanding world of subject matter, a subject matter of facts or information and of beliefs. This condition is satisfied only as the pastor views teaching and learning as a continuous process of reconstruction of experience. This condition in turn can be satisfied only as the pastor has a long look ahead, and views every present experience as a moving force in influencing what future experiences will be. I am aware that the emphasis I have placed upon church theory method may be misleading, for it may result only in calling up the special technique of theology research as that is conducted by specialists. But the meaning of the emphasis placed upon church method has more to do with specialized techniques. It means that church method is the only authentic means at our command for getting at the significance of our everyday experiences of the world in what we live. It means that church method provides a working pattern of the way in which and the conditions under which experiences are used to lead ever onward and outward. Adaptation of the method to child, young adult, and adult of various degrees of maturity is a problem for the pastor, and the constant factors in the problem are the formation of beliefs, acting upon believe, observation of the conditions which result, and organization of facts and beliefs for future use. Neither the beliefs, nor the activities, nor the observations, nor the church are the same for a person six years old as they are for one twelve or eighteen years old, to say nothing of the adult members. But at every level there is an expanding development of experience if experience is church in effect. Consequently, whatever the level of experience, we have no choice but either to operate in accord with the pattern it provides or else to neglect the place of intelligence in the development and control of a living and moving experience. This conclusion like the book as a whole, is anthropocentric and not a compendium of public worship, and, as space is not limited, the Church's prayer is represented here by content and not by structure. But it should be understood that each of the individual who prayer of help, believe, hope, and faith, as definite Christianity. This is most obviously the case where the prayer is, for example, a snatch of Old Testament prophecy which, one placed in a Christian liturgical setting, is drawn into the full light of revelation. The prayers of the Church are the voice of the Messianic people. This is a corporate voice in which everything is human finds utterance, in such a way that one speaks with the voice of all, and speak with the voice of each one. The anthropocentric was gathered together by a group of Christians of different denominations, so, understandably, the majority of the prayers included some from Christian sources. However, we have had the advantage of consultation with people of other traditions, who are practitioners of prayer and meditation. We recognize that it is as outsiders that we have chosen to listen to other prayers for the better of the world. That we have not given them equal space is not because we did not desire to do so, but because we had not the experience or Christian knowledge of God. My prayer for the universe of the world: Our Father God, our Lord Jesus Christ, and the Holy Spirit, grace, and peace be with us all. O my Lord God, who created us even though there was no cause for you to do so at any time; glory to you, O my Lord God, who called us your living image and likeness; glory to you, my Lord God, who nurtured us in freedom as rational beings; glory to you, O just Father, whose love was please to fashion us; glory to you, O holy Son Jesus Christ, who put on our flesh and saved us; glory to you, O living Spirit, who enriched us with your gifts; glory to you, O hidden nature, who revealed yourself in our manhood, and womanhood; glory to you, O my Lord Jesus Christ, who brought us to the knowledge of your God-head; glory to you, O my Lord Jesus Christ, who made us rational instruments for your service; glory to you, O my Lord Jesus Christ, who invited us to the exalted habitation of heaven; glory to you, O my Lord Jesus Christ, who taught us the ordering of the heavenly beings; glory to you, O my Lord Jesus Christ, who held us worthy to glorify you together with the angels; glory to you from every mouth, Father, Son and Holy Spirit, from those above and those below; glory to you Trinity; in both world glory to you, from both spiritual beings and from those in the body, from everlasting unto everlasting. Amen.

Prayer is relationship with God. Such relationship presupposes communication from both Religious. Not only does a person pray to God in words or unspoken thoughts, but also God communicates with the person in intuitions, often so clear that they can be interpreted into direct speech. At such times God's initiative is clearly apparent, and the heart is moved to respond in prayer or silent worship, or in inspired and obedient word or action. So it will be understood that there is not available the same prayer from which are communication to God. Yet there is enough available to give Christians he taster or feeling of the prayers of other religious man and woman perhaps provide evidence that if others can pray such prayers of beauty and devotion they must have some experience of the transcendent reality with which those praying are hoping to enter into loving communion, by whatever name they my call that Supreme God. There is the further expectation that as a man and woman in different traditions get to know each other better they will be able to share their spiritual treasures, and further still the hope that they may be able to pray some of the prayers of others belief. I pray to God to bless all of us. I am God's creature and my fellow is God's creature. My work is in the world, country, town, and his work is in the church. As we rise early for our work and He rises early for his work. Just as He does his presume to do his work, so I do presume to do my work. Will you say, I do much and He does great work. One may do much or one may do little; it is all one, provided he directs his heart to heaven.

Chapter 10

Experience the means and Goal of Christianity

To the reader who has followed this account of Religion and Christianity, subject throughout the long journey to the present page, it is possible to understand their problem in your life. With the words of God you may develop your own personal relationship with the Lord Jesus Christ and mankind, while strengthening your social and spiritual relationship in your home and community and in your church. With the word you may test your own standards, bring your own words and thoughts to God words and thoughts. God's saying to Isaiah, "For my thoughts are not your thoughts, neither are your ways my ways, saith the Lord. For as the heavens are higher than the earth, so are my ways higher than your ways, and my thoughts than your thoughts". To really study this book, you should pursue specific subjects from one subject to another. Be willing to put aside your own presupposition and opinions, and humbly ask, God to teach you. Never open this book for study without prayer for guidance and humility of heart and understanding. Regard this book as different from all others book, except the Holy Bible, inspired word of God. The mind will be turned toward spiritual things and will be less vulnerable to carnal things. Then you discover the sweetness of brief study with your husband, or your wife or your family and friend. The home altar will become a joy, it will be more precious than necessary food. Search the Scriptures, for in them ye think ye have eternal life;

and they are they which testify of me. So say the Lord Jesus Christ. In what I have said I have taken for granted the soundness of the principle that Christianity in order to accomplish its ends both for the individual learner and for society must be based upon experience which is always the actual life experience of some individual. I have argued for the acceptance of this principle nor attempted to justify it. Conservatives as well as radicals in church are profoundly discontented with the present church situation taken as a whole. There is at least this much agreement among intelligent persons of both theology of Christianity teachings. The Church must move one way or another, either backward to the intellectual and moral standards of a Christian age or forward to ever greater utilization of Christian method in the development of the possibilities of growing, expanding experience. I have but endeavored to point out some of the conditions which must be satisfactorily fulfilled if church takes the latter course. For I am so confident of the potentialities of church when it is treated as intelligently directed development of the possibilities inherent in ordinary experience that I do feel it necessary to criticize here the other route nor to advance arguments in favor of taking the route of experience. The only ground for anticipating failure in taking this path resides to my mind in the danger that experience and the experimental method will not be adequately conceived. There is discipline in the world so severe as the discipline of experience subjected to the tests of intelligent development and direction. Hence the only ground I can see for even a temporary reaction against the standards, aims, and methods of the newer church is the church is the failure of pastor who professedly adopt them to be faithful to them in practice. As I have emphasized more once, the road of the Christianity is not an easier one to follow that the Religion but a more strenuous and difficult one. It will remain so until if has attained its majority and that attainment will require many years of serious cooperative work on the part of its adherents. The greatest danger that attends its future is, the theory that it is an easy way to follow, so easy that its course may be improvised, if not in an impromptu fashion, at least almost from day to day or from week to week. It is for this reason that instead of extolling its principles, I have confined myself to showing certain conditions which must be fulfilled if it is to have the successful career which by right belongs to it. I have used frequently in what precedes the words

"Pastor" and "experience" church. I do not wish to close, however, without recording my firm belief that the fundamental issue is not of new versus Old Religion nor of progressive against traditional beliefs but a question of what anything whatever must be to be worthy of the name Christianity. I am not, I hope and believe, in favor of any ends or any methods simply because the name progressive may be applied to them. The basic question concerns the nature of church with no qualifying adjectives prefixed. What we want and need is Christianity pure and simple, and we shall make surer and faster progress when we devote ourselves to finding out just what Christianity is and what conditions have to be satisfied in order that Christianity may be a reality and not a name or a slogan. It is for this reason alone that I have emphasized the need for a sound philosophy of experience. As I previous stated that, as I have emphasized more once, the road of the Christian is not an easier one to follow than the Religion. The Jews worship without a temple. It is tribute to Israel's tenacity and vitality that the Mosaic faith not only survived this transition but was immeasurably deepened and enriched thereby. In Babylonia, may Jews must have capitulated to the pressures of culture and were soon absorbed into the general population. But others were bound more closely to their Jewish past and to the Jewish community. Indeed, it is phenomenal that the faith of Israel was preserved with great purity and zeal in the Babylonian exile, in contrast to the Egyptian exile where the religious heritage was corroded with alien ideas and practices, as can be seen from the Elephantine papyri. The great prophets had paved the way for the new expression of Christian faith by writing that God was not the Temple of Jerusalem. In Jeremiah's letter to the exiles, he wrote that even in a faraway land, where there was no God temple, men could have access to God through prayer. Read, Jer. 29:12-14. Pastor today are like Jeremiah recognition that the truth is in the relationship and that which is attested by the heart is the content of the relationship with God. God said, "I will be found by you". Jeremiah's insight contains not merely the simple paradox of the Sermon on the Mount, "Seek, and ye shall find", but also the anticipation of the Fourth Gospel written: "Jesus saith unto her, woman, believe me, the hour cometh, when ye shall neither in this mountain, nor yet at Jerusalem, worship the Father. Ye worship ye know not what: we know what we worship: for salvation is of the Jews. But the hour cometh, and now is, when the true worshippers shall worship the Father in spirit and in truth: for the Father seeketh such to worship him". John 4:21-23. In short, Jeremiah is telling the people in exile that, as a existentialist philosopher, wrote in 1889-1976 name Martin put it, "Homecoming is the return into the proximity of the source", not a return to Jerusalem; and that exile is the journey into far countries of the self-centered mind, not a long sojourn in Babylon. The question is the same today. "You shall not cease, O clamour, until upon the sands I shall have sloughed off every human allegiance. And in a passage in Deuteronomy, written either in exile or more probably shortly before, we read:

"And the Lord shall scatter you among the nations, and ye shall be left few in number among the heathen, whither the Lord shall lead you. And there ye shall serve gods, the work of men's hands, wood and stone, which neither see, nor hear, nor eat, nor smell. But if from thence thou shalt seek the Lord thy God, thou shalt find him, if thou seek him with all thy heart and with all thy soul. Deut. 4:27-29. In the exile, then, the people realized that they could turn to God anywhere With the confidence that He would be near, and that He would be their sanctuary in a foreign land. Undoubtedly a number of the prayers now found in the book of Psalms were composed during the Exile by unknown men who, like Jeremiah in his confessions, cried to God "out of depths" in Psalms 130. Moreover, during this period Jews undoubtedly came together in small groups, after the manner of the elders who consulted Ezekiel in his house, to be instructed in their Scriptural traditions and to worship in formally. It has often been suggested that the synagogue, the bringing together. As the Greek word "synagogue" means, for worship and teaching may have originated during the Exile. There is no evidence, however, that there were any organized local assemblies. All that we find and safely to said is that the later synagogues, which came to be scattered throughout the countries of the Dispersion, arose in response to a need that was first experience during the Exile, when Jews were separated from their land and their Temple. Even though the people were no longer held together by national allegiance they did have a common history and they had received a tradition. Like Isaiah in his time of discouragement, they devoted themselves to preserving the Torah until God's face would no longer be hidden from Israel. They studied and searched the tradition intensively for its meaning and carefully preserved their sacred lore in writing for future generations. Of course, not all the exiles were trained for this special task. But some of them, like Ezekiel, were preacher who either knew the tradition by heart, as was common in the ancient Orient, or who had brought along with them from Jerusalem some of the sacred writings as the most precious part of their light baggage. The people were accustomed to look to the preacher for exposition of Israel's faith. They relied especially on a class of preachers known as Levites, the descendants of Moses tribe of Levi. Before the Exile, these Levites had not always been preacher celebrants at the alter. Many of them were "teaching preacher", read II Chron. 15:3;17:9, and 35:3. This include us today in the twentieth century. The vocation was to give the people torah, or teaching about the ways in which God was to be worshiped and saved. Although the Levites lost some prestige as a result of Josiah reform, who the Lord supports, a King of Judah in the 7th cent. B.C., which gave great power to the preacher of the Jerusalem Temple, it is safe to assume that preacher instruction was continued in the Temple and later was resumed during the Exile. After the Jews experience the Exile, the most distinctive feature of the Jewish people is their sense of history. In many respects, the Jews have always been diverse in theology, in culture, and even in racial characteristics. But Judaism is the religion of a people who have a unique memory that reaches back through the centuries to the stirring events of their Bible, events that formed them as a people with a sense of identity and vocation. When the Passover is celebrated, whenever the Law is read in the synagogue, whenever a parent instructs his child in the tradition, this memory is kept alive. Indeed, if historical memory were destroyed, the Jewish community would soon dissolve. Christians, too, have this historical sense. The Christian church is diverse culturally, socially and to some extent theologically; but it is also a distinctive community with a long memory that reaches back through the Christian ages to the crucial events of which the Bible is the record and witness. To be sure, Christian remembrance focuses especially on the coming of Jesus, the Christ, His life, death, and resurrection. As a Christian myself, memory this event is viewed as the fulfillment of the historical drama of Israel set forth in the Jewish Bible, which in Christian circles in known as the "Old Testament". These writings represent the literary deposit of the memory upon which two of world's great religions are based. Judaism and Christianity differ in their interpretation of these historical experiences, but they agree on the unique character of the history with which the Old Testament deals. Let us look at Judaism: the term is sometimes used of every form of Jewish religion after the destruction of Solomon's Temple in 586 B. C. It seems better to confine it to the period beginning with the destruction of Herod's temple in A. D. 70, except where the phenomena under discussion can be clearly traced back to the A.D. 70 period. In this period, unless the context clearly demands otherwise, it will be further restricted to that form of Judaism, it is generally called Rabbinic, Traditional or Orthodox period. As I stated, the restriction of sacrifice to Jerusalem by Josiah, the destruction of the temple in 586 B.C., and the growing dispersion of Jewry both east and west meant a fundamental change in religious outlook. Though theoretically the culture in Jerusalem remained the center of Jewish Religion, at least eighty per cent of the people were not able to make effective use of it. The only one of the many attempted answers to this problem that concerns us here was the making of a strict observance of the law the major concern of all Jews. The Pre-Christian Elements in Judaism: (1) The Jews; (2) The Torah; (3) The Oral Law; (4) The Messiah; (5) The Resurrection. After the developments after A. D. 70; the first efforts of the Rabbis were to preserve Judaism by creating a monolithic body. On the one hand they expelled dissident elements, frowned on Gnostic speculation and reduced the area of individual freedom. On the other they so transformed certain basic areas of Jewish thought as to make acceptance of Jesus as Messiah and Saviour virtually impossible. (1) Uniformity; (2) The Doctrine of God; (3) The Doctrine of Man; (4) Sin, Sacrifice and Mediation; (5) Merit. The basic fact of Judaism religion is to service of God than knowledge of him. Most of vital modern Orthodox Judaism has been influenced by it; in Western Europe the influences of the Renaissance and modern thought did not reach them, with few exceptions, until about the time of the French Revolution, and in Eastern Europe and Moslem lands much later. The Conservative Jew has trimmed away those commandments which seem to have lost their meaning. The Reform Jew mean "Liberal", in Britain, places the Prophets [Man of God], before the Torah and retains only those customs of the past which he can rationalize. Because of the inheritance of Christianity from Judaism was a Scripture. Jesus in his preaching constantly referred to this Scripture, and the disciples followed him in this practice. They accepted as a Christian fact which directly concerned them the existence among the Jews of a body of writings received as sacred and authoritative. This body of writing did not profess to include all the religious books that had appeared during the history of the Jewish people; and other religion. It did not include all the religious documents which were in circulation among the Jews at the period; this include other religious too. It was a body of writings which had been brought together by a process of selection, given an authority not possessed by their other religious literature, and invested with a sanctity which set it apart as in some particular way connected with the official religious life of the people. In this there was nothing unique; we find the same factors at work among other peoples producing the sacred books of other religions. We find in such cases as the Manichaean are to some extent obscure, though it is obviously connected with the Persian Manes in A.D. 215-75, who in the middle of the third century proclaimed himself a prophet, enunciated his new doctrine and was finally executed. So far they are known to us, his views, which are thought to derive from a Nazoraeans, and Christians of St. John, Mandaeans are adherents of Mandaism, which is now confined to a few small communities South of Bagdad. The Book of John, are a strange amalgam of myth mean "unknown" history and ritual where teachings of rabbinic Judaism are mingled inconsistently with Gnostic Manichaeanism and with traces of Christianity. Man's soul, tortured by demons, is imprisoned within the body, from which only a divine being, Manda d'hayye a Hebrew mean "knowledge of life", can release him. Frequent baptisms are required to prepare the soul for its ascent. Theories have been advanced, notably by Lidzbarski and Bultmann, claming John as the founder of the sect, whose myths were later interwoven with primitive Christianity, especially by the writer of the Fourth Gospel. Uncertainty in dating the literature, and the intrinsic religious worthlessness of it, suggest that Mandaism borrowed and debased Christian traditions and vice versa. During the early centuries of the life of the Christian church, the Christian, striving to express the meaning of his or her faith, might have abandoned the Old Testament religion, admitting that time makes ancient good uncouth, had he or she not possessed a boundless veneration for the mysterious wisdom of the past, as well as methods of reinterpreting that wisdom and of making it comprehensible for his or her own times. Some of these methods of interpretation were traditional in the Judaism out of which Christianity arose; others were gifts of the Hellenistic school, and others were standards of interpretation ultimately developed within the church itself. Let us first consider Jewish methods of exegesis. Within the Old Testament we can trace the reinterpretation of the cardinal events of religious history. Along with a progressive revelation went a progressive interpretation, especially in the writings of the prophets. We find that the prophets themselves were reinterpreted in the works of the apocalyptic writer of Judaism. Not the Old Testament as we view it in the light of historical research, but the Old Testament explained by apocalyptic interpretation, was the Bible of the earliest church. The goal of Christianity is to understand the Bible from its text alone, but from the mass of legends and legal decisions which had gathered about it in the previous two or three centuries. The stories are usually called "haggada", under this heading may be classified all the nonlegal interpretations of Scripture. Beside them stood the "halakah", interpretations by which the Scriptures could be made to govern every detail of Jewish civil and religious life. Both types of exegesis are found in early Christianity. Both are based on the literal meaning of a text, usually taken out of context, but never contradicted. For in Jewish eyes the whole Bible was verbally inspired by God. There could be no question of contradiction or error. Not all Jews, however, were completely true to their inherited tenets. Those who lived outside Palestine had a tendency to make the Bible say what their more enlightened neighbors said. They admired the, assured results, of Greek philosophy and wanted to enjoy a synthesis between philosophy and religion. The most prominent "modernist" of ancient Judaism was Philo of Alexandria. While he once called Jerusalem his native "city", his intellectual life was largely centered in Hellenistic Alexandria. It was there that forerunners whom he occasionally mentions had learned to interpret the Old Testament allegorically. The allegorical method is as old as the rise of Greek philosophy, and probably owes its existence to it. Many of philosopher who studies the Bible interpretation of the cardinal events of that religious point. So also a Jews, reading his Greek Old Testament and finding it full of anthropomorphic expressions, might come to believe that God had spoken to men through symbols and dark sayings. And he would observe the fact that the heroes of the Old Testament, like those of Homer, lived on a different plane from men of his own time. This apply to a Christian reading his King James Version of the Holy Bible finding the same anthropomorphic expressions in his Bible too. Their lives seemed simpler. They must have been types or examples. And an etymological analysis of their names might prove to the analyst, if to no one else, that they were really personified virtues. I makes such a study and it is so unconvincing that recent critics have doubted his knowledge of the Hebrew language. Remember, the allegorical method has very little rational justification, but it was highly popular in antiquity. It made possible the retention of Homer as a schoolbook in spite of the criticism of the intelligentsia. Within Christianity and Judaism it was the first line of defense for the Old Testament. Even as early as the first century the method is used at least twice. The first and more famous instance is found in Gal. 4:21-24 read, "Tell me, ye that desire to be under the law, do ye not hear the law? For it is written, that Abraham had two sons, the one by a bondmaid, the other by a freewoman. But he who was of the bondwoman was born after the flesh; but he of the freewoman was by promise. Which things are an allegory: for these are the two covenants; the one from the mount Sinai, which gendereth to bondage, which is Agar". Now this is an allegory: "these women are two covenants" Here Paul, interpreting the history of the Old Testament as full of types or examples for us, whatever was written in former days was written for our instruction. See Romans 15:4, goes so far as to use the Greek word for "allegory". These things, he says, were meant allegorically by the writers of scripture. Modern readers may doubt the accuracy of Paul's exegesis; but in its day it made the Old Testament meaningful for many Greek speaking Jews and Christians today. The other example is in the Revelation of John. As a whole, this apocalypse is written in a style and form intentionally enigmatic. In a description of the fall of the great city Jerusalem, the author John explains that allegorically it is called Sodom and Egypt, for the Lord was crucified there in Rev. 11:8. He knows that in his Old Testament Jerusalem is sometimes called "Sodom" because of its wickedness in Isa. 1:9: he himself contributes the identification with Egypt. To understand Christianity you much understand the Old

Testament Religion mean Judaism. Most of the New Testament writers stand close to Judaism and interpret the Old Testament literally. Nevertheless there is a certain air of freedom about their exegesis which is not found among the rabbis. Where does this freedom come from? It comes from Jesus Christ himself. Jesus was the creator of Christian biblical interpretation. His exegesis has within it a double attitude to his Bible, though later interpreter develop only single aspects of his thought. This double relationship to the Old Testament has troubled commentators on the Gospels since ancient times. On the one hand, Jesus Christ takes the Old Testament as it stands and insists on its permanent authority. On the other, he ventures to criticize it, to reinterpret it, to attack not only tradition interpretations but even scripture itself. Is not such an attitude paradoxical? By critical methods can we get rid of one or the other aspect of Jesus interpretation? Unfortunately, only an arbitrary criticism can water down the difficulty which we face. Good attested that the Lord prove that his relationship to the Jewish scriptures was bipolar. Brought up in a conservative Jewish family, he respected the authority of the law. To a man or woman who wanted to "inherit eternal life", Jesus Christ quoted the second table of the Decalogue in Mark. 10:19. He could attack the tradition of the Pharisees by claiming that they abandoned the "commandment of God" in Mark. 7:8-9. While there were those who argued that he was destroying the law, he could be remembered as saying that he intended only to reinterpret it. His aim was revitalization, not destruction. David was not the only writer of Scripture to speak in the Holy Spirit in Mark 12:36; Moses and the other prophets must have spoken or written in the spirit as well. The testimony of the Spirit could not be rejected. At the same time, the New Testament as a whole, the Old Testament is treated as a book of hope. Christians, following the example of Jesus Christ and building upon it, gradually came to reject the Jewish law as law. But since it was the inspired word of God, it must "they believed", contain a deeper meaning. This meaning they found in types of Jesus and of his Church. "As Moses lifted up the serpent in the wilderness, so must the Son of Man be lifted up" in John 3:14. The author of I Peter expresses the normal Christian belief that the prophets could not be understood without the spirit of Christ in I Peter 1:10-11; II Cor. 3:12-18. Although, Jesus bring Christianity has sprung from the faith that in its founder God was made

97

manifest in the flesh and dwelt among men. Other religions have developed a conception of incarnation, but none has given it such centrality. In the belief that Jesus Christ is the clearest portrayal of the character of God all the rest of Christian doctrine is implied. It is not easy to tell the story briefly and clearly. The Christian century has had more books written about it than any other comparable period of history. The Judaism sources bearing on its history and the Gospels and Epistles of the New Testament, and these again we must make a comparative statement have been more thoroughly searched by inquiring minds than any other books ever written. Many historical criticism has been particularly busy with them during the last one hundred years and has reached the verdict that in the New Testament the early Christian belief about Jesus Christ the Son of God has overlaid and modified the record of the beliefs of Jesus himself, his own faith, but there is no unanimity about the degree of modification. It is known that Jesus himself did not write down his teachings but relied upon his disciples to go about preaching what he taught. It is generally assumed by historians that after his death some of them did write down his sayings, with occasional notes of the historical setting, before they should be forgotten, and that thus a document or group of documents, came into being that scholars call "Q", was colored by the prepossessions of the early Christians and had saying added to it that were mistakenly ascribed to Jesus Christ, but on the whole it was authentic and quite naturally became primary source material for the compilers of St. Matthew and St. Luke. These compilers used a great deal of other material also, both oral and written; for example they drew much of their material from St. Mark, already existent (65-70 A.D.). If you will known that the Gospel of St. John was not written until the end of the century and then largely from concern with the theological implications of Jesus Christ life and death. Through all of these records runs the often unseen division between what is from Jesus himself and what is from the Apostolic Age. But when scholars are asked to separate the material that authentically reveals the historical Jesus Christ from the material that reflects the growing Christology of the early Christians, they vary widely in their interpretations. At certain points each Christians is thrown back, after careful study, upon his own judgment, even his intuitive feeling in deciding what is from the historical Jesus Christ and what is from the early church. In many cases these decisions on the quality of the evidence are crucial. There is some warrant therefore for saying that every life of Jesus Christ is in some sense a confession fideism mean, the belief that faith alone is the basis of knowledge rather than reason; or, at the very least, a personal impression of what actually happened. Remember, it was Jesus Christ whom bring Christianity. That Jesus was born into a part of the world that had only recently been brought under Roman dominion is of some significance, to begin with. One of the last acquisitions of Roman arms was Palestine. The Jews, as we have seen in the Bible history dealing with them, had been subjected over and over to a foreign yoke, yet the Roman rule came to seem more intolerable than any. This was due in large part to the fact that the Romans were an aloof, administrative group. They had in particular a purely regulatory feeling concerning local people; there was no fellow feeling at all. It had been different with the Greeks, who were an imaginative and responsive people, able to enter into the spirit of a locality and weigh its ideas as though they deserved respect. But the Jews and the Romans were poles apart. There was so little of seeing eye to eye that they were enigmas to each other and gave up trying to arrive at an understanding. This hardening of the heart toward each other's natures and cultures precluded any possibility of adjustment and therefore made it inevitable that their living together in the same land would produce social tumult. This was so much the case throughout Palestine that in his childhood, Jesus Christ must have gained little better than a confusing impression of swift political and social changes taking place all around him. Jesus grew up in an atmosphere of argument, conflict, and bitterness. There was endless talk. Older minds were bewildered like today, by events and torn by mounting tensions. Even now the historians picture of the periods remains confusing. To the Christians of today in this century, the events that followed the death of Jesus Christ were of greater importance than those that preceded it. It was true for them and it is true for us, that the life and teachings of Jesus Christ were of priceless value for their daily life and thought; yet his resurrection from the dead was of higher value still, for it was their proof of living reality as a person, that is, as the undying Lord of life who was the assurance of their own immortality and the pledge of their unbreakable spiritual oneness with God the Father. We who are a Christians the resurrection was the proof of the truth of the Gospel, and descent of the Holy Spirit at Pentecost was the guarantee that the power that was in Jesus Christ is in us too. The Disciple now took courage and began preaching boldly in the streets where but a few weeks before Jesus Christ encountered an opposition that had ended in his crucifixion. As you may know that they met with startling success. Hundreds of converts joined them. The Pharisees and Sadducees in alarm arrested St. Peter and St. John, brought them before the Sanhedrin, and ordered them to cease speaking as they did in the name of Jesus Christ, St. Peter and the Apostles, we read, answered: We must obey God rather than men". For some time ago Theudas appeared, claiming to be a person of importance, and a group of men numbering some four hundred joined him. But he was killed and all his followers were dispersed and disappeared. After Jesus resurrection, two factors seem to have saved the church from annihilating persecution; first, the Disciple were followers of a dead leader and might be expected to lose their fervor with the passage of time, and second, the Disciple obviously kept all the provisions of the Jewish Law. In fact, the Palestinian followers of Jesus Christ went daily to the Temple and honored the Law of Moses as much as any Jew, requiring circumcision of every convert not already circumcised, as if they were just a Jewish sect. But remember they had made some unorthodox additions to the accepted faith and practice. They also believed that Jesus Christ was the Messiah foretold by Isaiah and that he would shortly reappear on the clouds of heaven as the Son of Man. We also should noted that Jesus Christ, according to Christians, realized in his own life and death this ideal of the Servant of God suffering and dying for the sins of mankind. Second Chapter of Isaiah through his monotheism furnished the basis for the theology of Judaism, Christianity, and Islam. His interpretation of suffering, its purifying and redeeming effect on Israel and through them on the world, made the atoning suffering and death of Jesus Christ cannot be fully understood without Second Chapter of Isaiah. We find that Isaiah is the most evangelical of the prophets. He also passed on to all humanity the element of hope, the outlook on a coming Golden Age and the doctrine of the Kingdom of God on earth; to which all men without distinction of race are called. The Jewish and Christians met in private homes, such as the home of John Mark's mother in Jerusalem, for group gatherings, which devoted to the breaking of bread and prayers. The believers shared everything they had with one another, sold their property and belonging, and divided the proceeds according to their special needs, and they all had a vigorous proselyting spirit and baptized their converts. But Paul has been frequently called "the second founder of Christianity". Certain it is that Paul withstood and silenced the Judaizers mean "tradition", who thereafter steadily lost importance in the Christian movement, but more important, Paul developed certain basic theological concepts for stating the spiritual effects of Jesus upon the lives of his follower, concepts that enabled Christianity to win the Gentile world. To that world he brought intact the Christianity of Jesus himself in the vehicle of a faith about Jesus Christ as Lord. Sometime we need to look at oneself to understand your faith and belief. Paul on the other hand, he accomplished only after an early career of fierce opposition to Christianity. He was a non-Palestinian Jew, born, about the same time as Jesus, in the town of Tarsus in Cilicia, then an important city and the seat of a university where the Stoic and Cynic philosophies were taught. We find that he learned something of the Greek mystery cults and the desire of their adherents to achieve immortality by identification with dying and rising savior-gods. His family was apparently well off, and presumably had purchased Roman citizenship; he therefore had he legal status of a free born Roman man. But he reacted adversely to the religious ideas of his Hellenistic environment and remained a strict Pharisee. Filled with an earnest desire for "the righteousness which is from the Law", he went to Jerusalem and sat at the feet of Gamaliel, the leading Pharisaic teacher. Of this period of his life he later wrote: "I surpassed many of my own age among my people in my devotion to Judaism, I was so fanatically devoted to what my forefathers had handed down". Paul joined furiously in the persecution of the early Christians. He was present as an approving spectator at the stoning of Stephen. When the Christian believers fled northward to Damascus and beyond, Paul went to the high priest and asked for letters to the synagogues in Damascus, where he probably lived; so that if he found any men or women there who belonged to the way, he might bring them in chains to Jerusalem. Read the book of Acts; "as he was approaching Damascus, a sudden light flashed around him from heaven, and he fell to the ground. Then he heard a voice saying to him, "Saul! Why do you persecute me? He was blinded by the bright vision, Paul was led by the hand into Damascus, where for three days he could not see and neither ate nor drank. He believed that the resurrected Jesus Christ, in whom the Christians now centered their faith, had appeared also to him. This is why we believe in Jesus Christ the Son of God had been raised from the dead so that He might soon return on the clouds with his Father who should judge the world. So vast a change in Paul's life was now made necessary that he went off into upper Arabia to think things through. Then he returned to Damascus. Paul became a Christian leader not only there but also far to the north at Antioch, the third largest city in the roman empire, where the new Christian was making many converts among the Gentiles. This why we are Christian not religion; if you was born again, you are a Christian because you believed in the Son of God. Jesus saying to Nicodemus, "Verily, verily, I say unto thee, Except a man be born again, he cannot see the kingdom of God". John 3:3. We came to know the freedom of the Spirit during the days of your conversion. Most Christians were for the more part uncircumcised and without the knowledge of the God's Law. In there great hunger to know the secret of true righteousness, they only condition of a good life enjoying the Lord Jesus Christ favor. They will be surprised and delighted to discover that those who followed Jesus Christ will, quite apart from the Religion belief, more profoundly good than those who obeyed other Religious. Furthermore, the righteousness that we in Jesus Christ are greater than the righteousness that was from other religious. The reason is that Jesus Christ changed your life inward disposition and gave you the right relationship to his fellow Christians and to God, so that He did what is right from the heart, without having to refer constantly to outward legal requirements. Remember, love is the fulfillment of the Law and Christianity. Therefore the weary bondage of the Law could be cast aside for the freedom of the Spirit. There is no further need. It is very in possible that you know that, it was at some point that the "Judaizers" came into conflict with Paul. He had it out with Peter, James and John at Jerusalem. In Galatians 1; and 2, Paul implies that obedience to Jewish law had become so critical an issue that, after fourteen years, Paul felt impelled to explain to the Jerusalem preacher the message he preached to the Gentiles. By God's power, Paul claimed, he had been made an apostle to the Gentiles, just as Peter was an apostle to the Jews.

Peter, James and John accepted Paul message and mission and shook hands, asking only that Christians in the Gentile world remember the needy in Jerusalem. To understand other religious belief and secular worldviews and their practical meaning we have to picture in mind of things that they believe. We have to enter into the lives of those for whom such ideas and actions are important. Some says, "Never judge a person until you have walked a mile in his or her shoes". In understand religions we should define religion narrowly. It is important for us to recognize secular ideologies as part of the story of Christianity. It is not impossible to divide Religion from Christianity, partly because they sometimes function in society like religions, and partly because the distinction between Religion and Christianity beliefs and practices in Jesus Christ. Our space is at the end. Perhaps this book here unfolder suggests that basic Christianity is not an escape from the world into solitariness, but a way of sending one's life for others in order to find it; not a retreat into ultimate truth, but a redemptive mission, a way of salvation leading into the world and for the world.

CONCLUSION

To the reader who has followed this account of Religion and Christianity, subject throughout the long journey to the present page, it is possible to understand their subject in your daily life. With the words of God you may develop your own personal relationship with the Lord Jesus Christ, while strengthening your faith and spiritual relationship in your home, community and in your church. With the word of God you may test your own standard, bring your own words and thoughts to God thought. To really study this book, you should pursue specific subjects from one subject to another. Be willing to put aside your own presupposition and opinions, and humbly ask, God to teach you. Never open the Holy Bible and this book for study without prayer for guidance and humility of heart and understanding. Regard this book as different from all others book, except the Holy Bible, inspired word of God. Author goal is that readers may be able to open King James Version translations of the Holy Bible introduced here and immediately find themselves at church, home, quite familiar with the territory. That explains why I have given generous samples of each of the documents, in the theory that once readers have worked their way through the specified passages, they will have a model for further study on their own. Admittedly, I have a second goal, which should be exposed. I place a very high value on Christianity set forth here, which I conceive to take their place at the heights of humanity's intellectual achievement and heritage. Sheer love of the writing made me want to share with the readers a some sample of a vast treasury of knowledge, learning, beauty of God's word, but, above all,

God love us all. Here is Christians, beyond Scripture Jesus Christ, for all to see. This book does not pretend to objectivity on the intellectual excellence and spiritual quality of what is book. I cannot imagine any reader of these pages who would want things any other way. In this way, readers immediately see how I conceive discourse to be constructed, being able to compare the formal traits of one whole unit of thought with another, one cogent but contingent proposed unit with another, and so on upward. This is the book that I have always wanted to write. But it has taken me a long time to do it, nearly thirty seven years, from the day of 1971, was studies at university study philosophy twenty one, found my intellectual ability. The first genuinely interesting set of intellectual problems I had encountered, myself, the most consistently compelling ones I ever addressed. Remember, the study of the Bible is an ever expanding frontier. To open the Bible is to enter a world that is strange to the modern mind. It is disconcerting to discover that some of our questions such as the existence of God lie outside or inside Biblical concern. Because of the tension between Religion and Christianity outlook and the modern world view, the interpreter is constantly pushed toward the realm of apologetics the intellect defense of the validity of Christianity truth. This book is written with an awareness of that tension, and with the conviction that Christianity message about life's meaning makes a claim upon us in the twentieth century. But before one can face such questions squarely, we must first understand the Bible on its own terms, in so far as we can. And that is the aim of this book. Christian's faith is radically historical, for it rests upon the conviction that God's revelation His Son is mediated through historical experience of which the Bible is the record and the witness. Historical study is indispensable to Christians and Religion historical faith. In the Old Testament we do not deal with timeless truths that are related only incidentally to historical circumstances, but with truth that is inseparably related to specific times, places, and peoples. Our task, then, is to try to understand the Biblical message in its dynamic context of Religion and Christianity, Criteria of Economic, Investments, and Receive wealth from God Blessing, and others benefits. We shall seek to enter into the concrete life situations out of which the various writing have come, and to understand what the writers were saying to their times. Toward their end, a series of study of title has been provide to help the reader familiarize himself or herself with the Biblical setting. A book of this kind is possible only because of the creative work of the King James Version, some of whom mentioned are the author. To simplify the presentation as much as possible; I have avoided carrying the reader for a field into scholarly debates, and have kept Scripture documentation to a maximum. In deference to Religion and Christians readers, references have been omitted to the works of many Religious scholars who have been pioneers in the fields of Biblical criticism and theology. Each of these Chapter, are from the King James Version, and I am constantly engaged in teaching the Bible, has made valuable suggestions for the improvement of this book. Also, I owe a great debt of thanks to God the Father, the Son Jesus Christ the Holy Spirit, and to my late father Rev. E.D. Blankenship Sr., and my late [Mother] Mrs. Blankenship, Dr. Herbert J. Vandort, and my [Wife] for their assistance and encouragement during the years when these volumes were taking shape. One of the most difficult problems in the Old Testament is the dating of events. This book is not intended as an introduction to the Old Testament in the technical sense which that world has acquired in scholarly circles. Rather, it aims to introduce the general reader to the Scriptural treasures that have profoundly influenced western civilization. In a day when world events urge us to face seriously the question of the meaning of human life, it is hoped that this book will help the reader understand what the Bible has to say. My philosophy is "If you want a good understanding of Christianity from a historical perspective, this is the book for you to acquire that knowledge". Let the book help us to value our belief more. It is not without purpose that God has so wonderfully inspired and preserved His message; it is not without purpose that He raised up His workers to search out the precious masterpiece, as the noblest and most beautiful book in the world. The Old Testament seems to have been accepted from the beginning as an authoritative revelation of God, and it was not very long before the writings which came ultimately to form the New Testament were also in circulation, carrying a similar, though not precisely assessed, authority. And now we have followed the book Religion and Christianity from the old Testament developed from c.1200 B.C., the only surviving portion of the national literature of early Israelites. The New Testament written during the 1st century A.D., and possibly the early 2d century. Remember, Judaism is the religion of the Jewish people, and may be defined as the belief in one God and the practical effect of that belief on life. Also, one of Judaism's chief principles is belief in God's choice of the Jews to preach His message, mean preach God "Word". From Judaism came Christianity in Jesus Christ, the Son of God. Historically speaking, Christian came to designate note a sect of Judaism, but a separate religion based on the person of Jesus Christ, rather than on a book of law, a dogma, or an institution. Christianity is design the Christian faith as founded on the life and teachings of Jesus Christ, and his Disciple. Though rooted in Judaism an entirely new Christianity, the new song, new heart, and new spirit. It is a revelation of God through His Son Jesus Christ; a way of life based on a personal experience of Jesus Christ. We who are Christian, we obedience to his commandments, and a determination to increase the brotherhood or sisterhood of his followers into a redeemed world society made up of perfected individuals.

Index of books of the bible

References are to Chapters
(All Biblical sources are from the King James Version Translation)

Reference